STUDIES IN BUSINESS EXPECTATIONS
AND PLANNING

DETERMINANTS OF CAPITAL EXPENDITURES

AN INTERVIEW STUDY

BY

ROBERT EISNER
Associate Professor of Economics
Northwestern University

PUBLISHED BY THE UNIVERSITY OF ILLINOIS, URBANA
1956

UNIVERSITY OF ILLINOIS
COLLEGE OF COMMERCE AND BUSINESS ADMINISTRATION

PAUL M. GREEN, *Dean*

BUREAU OF ECONOMIC AND BUSINESS RESEARCH

V LEWIS BASSIE, *Director*

CONTENTS

		PAGE
I.	Introduction — Some Epistemological Observations	7
II.	Scope and Method of the Study	12
III.	Analysis of Findings	15
	Nature and Extent of Forward Estimates and Capital Expenditure Plans	15
	Formal Aspects of Approval	19
	The Role of Expansion	21
	The Roles of Nonexpansionary Expenditures and of Replacement	25
	Price Considerations	26
	Supply of Money Capital	27
	Taxes	29
	Calculations	29
	Flexibility and Time Lags	34
	Accuracy of Estimates and Reaction to Surveys	35
	Conclusion	36
IV.	Individual Firm Reports	38
	Firm A (Farm Equipment)	38
	Firm B (Farm Equipment)	49
	Firm C (Steel)	53
	Firm D (Steel)	62
	Firm E (Beer)	64
	Firm F (Beer)	66
	Firm G (Containers)	69
	Firm H (Containers)	71
	Firm I (Shoes)	75
	Firm J (Shoes)	77
	Firm K (Rubber)	80
	Firm L (Rubber)	82
	Firm M (Rubber)	86
	Firm N (Rubber)	91

PREFACE

This monograph is the second in a series of studies carried out as part of a three-year research project on business expectations and planning, conducted under the over-all direction of Professor Franco Modigliani at the Bureau of Economic and Business Research of the University of Illinois in cooperation with the National Opinion Research Center of the University of Chicago. This project was financed primarily from a grant by the Merrill Foundation for Advancement of Financial Knowledge, matched in part by contributions in various forms by the University of Illinois.

The original interviews on which the present study is largely based were completed in 1951 and 1952. This work at the University of Illinois was supplemented after the author moved to Northwestern University by further research and additional data based on correspondence with interviewees and on a number of reinterviews between 1952 and 1955, undertaken with the assistance of a faculty research fellowship awarded by the Social Science Research Council. The writer is indebted, for valuable and generous advice and aid in various phases of this work, to V Lewis Bassie, Howard R. Bowen, Jean Bronfenbrenner Crockett, Jack Feldman, Robert Ferber, Paul M. Green, Richard B. Heflebower, C. Addison Hickman, Bert G. Hickman, Dexter M. Keezer, Ruth P. Mack, Owen H. Sauerlender, Robert P. Ulin, and in largest measure, Professor Modigliani. In addition, of course, he owes primary acknowledgment to the large number of necessarily anonymous company presidents, vice-presidents, controllers, and other officers, whose patient cooperation made this study possible.

The reader may wish to refer to a companion piece to this study, "Interview and Other Survey Techniques and the Study of Investment," *Problems of Capital Formation, Studies in Income and Wealth* (published by the Princeton University Press for the National Bureau of Economic Research, in press), Vol. XIX. That work includes a description and analysis of previous studies in this area, a brief summary of findings of the interviews analyzed herein (along with some scattered observations on investment in inventories which stem from the data of these interviews), and a few pages of "epistemological warning," which we have taken the liberty of reproducing herein.

Robert Eisner

I. INTRODUCTION
SOME EPISTEMOLOGICAL OBSERVATIONS

This monograph represents an attempt to synthesize interview data and economic theory in an area where the two have seemed painfully unreconciled. The writer has pursued his work in the stubborn belief that the basic theoretical analysis of business investment may well be enriched, elaborated, and modified but need not and should not be rejected. Consequently, his interviews of executives in 14 large manufacturing firms in the East and Midwest involved the solicitation of data to fit his largely preconceived structure. Lest the reader feel entirely helpless in making his own evaluation of material gathered in this fashion, many of the original interview data — the statements and opinions of the business executives themselves — are included in this paper. The reader may thus participate in the absorption — where possible — of the particularistic, atheoretical responses of practical men of affairs into useful places in a unified economic theory.

Certain serious methodological questions must be faced in any evaluation of findings obtained by interviewing individual businessmen or by subjecting them to questionnaire inquiries. These questions have, however, frequently been ignored or at least handled in perfunctory fashion.

First we must note that one cannot accept the respondents' descriptions or explanations of what they do without further examination. Economists asking questions are in some danger of grasping a new tool from psychologists without forewarning themselves of the pitfalls involved. It is quite possible that the individual businessman does not really know, in any sense satisfactory to the economist, what determines his investment decisions. We may add that if he did know he might not tell!

However, the businessman's possible lack of knowledge as to what, in some sense satisfactory to the inquiring economist, determines his actions may actually induce him to tell things that are not quite true. One may wonder, for example, whether the fairly numerous indications of formulas and calculations brought into evidence in the pages to follow may not betray above all a desire to satisfy (in fact, spuriously) *the economist's* desire for method and system. The businessman may be quite right in his original impulse to see his decisions as essentially particularistic in motivation and apparently almost random in character. Finding of common causes, generalizing, and theorizing by the economist may still be very useful and indeed essential. But the businessman's explanation of why he does things may not be the economist's.

One may wish to increase the weight attached to this last point when one considers certain problems of moving from the individual firm, on which individual businessmen focus their attention, to aggregative relations which receive major attention from economists. It is entirely probable that causative factors that loom large in individual decisions wash out in the aggregate. This point may perhaps be seen most clearly by considering the approach that an investigator should take to the problem of explaining or predicting the number of applicants accepted in medical schools. He might interview carefully selected samples of accepted and rejected applicants. Those rejected might ascribe their rejection (correctly) to such factors as poor undergraduate grades, lack of good letters of recommendation, studying at a relatively unknown college, or racial or religious discrimination. Those accepted might conversely explain their good fortune (also correctly) in terms of good grades, good letters, good schools, and desirable social attributes. Yet the aggregate number of students admitted to medical schools must depend in the short run on the facilities of these schools and in the long run on factors such as the effective demand of the community for medical services. Clearly the replies of accepted and rejected applicants in an interview (or questionnaire) survey of this kind might give information as to why certain applicants were accepted rather than others but it would tell us little about why so few (or so many) were accepted in the aggregate.

The contrived illustration above finds some very real parallels in the study of determinants of investment. For we are interested in factors determining the aggregate of investment rather than what may cause capital expenditures to be made at a certain time by one firm rather than another. A case in point may well be the answers received by the writer from executives of several firms on the role of accelerated depreciation of capital assets for tax purposes. As we shall note, some indication was found that businessmen considered such tax advantages an inducement to capital expenditures. Yet it should be clear that one would not be warranted in asserting on the basis of such a finding that an extension of accelerated amortization for tax purposes, or any similar tax concessions, would raise the aggregate of investment. It might well be that higher depreciation charges and their resultant effects upon income distribution, tax incidence, total tax receipts, and/or governmental expenditures might lower aggregate demand and lower its investment component.[1] In any event, this is a problem for the

---

[1] See Robert Eisner, "Accelerated Depreciation· Some Further Thoughts," *Quarterly Journal of Economics*, May, 1955.

economic analyst; the business respondents can furnish at best only a part of the material for a solution.

An example of exaggerated reliance upon interview findings to decide a major issue in the theory of investment is afforded by much of the discussion of the role of the rate of interest. For one of the most popular refrains of investigators who have reported the businessman's explanations of his own motivations as if they were the causes of economic phenomena has been the "debunking" of the rate of interest. This is not to argue that fluctuations in the rate of interest *are* an important cause of fluctuations in the rate of investment. But the contrary conclusion to which many investigators point,[2] that the rate of interest is quite *un*important, is frequently unwarranted by *their* findings.

This may be made clear by positing a model in which there are only two variables which may influence individual investment decisions: the aggregate rate of sales (or changes in the aggregate rate of sales) and the rate of interest. It may then be postulated further that although sales of individual firms may fluctuate by a substantial amount — say 10 percent — from year to year, there is no change in the aggregate rate of sales. Thus what one firm or industry gains another firm or industry must lose. Fluctuations in the rate of interest may be of similar magnitude — say 10 percent, as from 5 percent to 4½ percent — but being occasioned largely by actions of national monetary institutions show little difference in relative magnitude when looked at from individual and aggregative points of view.[3] If in such a situation businessmen were asked what causes them to alter their investment, or indeed if a cross-section or time series analysis were made on an individual basis, what answers might be expected as to the relative roles of interest rates and sales, demand, or profits? Clearly, interest costs would be a relatively minor factor in contemplated new investment by businessmen faced with changes in sales on the order of 10 percent and probably greater consequent changes in profits. Yet just as clearly, on the aggregative level, changes in the rate of sales would have nothing to do with changes in the rate of investment (there would be no change in aggregate sales), as would be confirmed by statistical analysis of aggregative time series data for an economy conforming to our assumption. On the other hand, fluctuations in the rate of interest, which on

---

[2] See "Interview and Other Survey Techniques and the Study of Investment," *Studies in Income and Wealth* (Princeton: Princeton University Press, in press), Vol XIX.

[3] There may, of course, be certain changes in the structure of interest rates. However, the consequent variation in incidence as between firms would be relatively small.

the individual firm level seemed of too minor weight to merit mention, are the only factor with any significance on the aggregative level.

Now, of course, in the real world we do not have economies in which there is no change in aggregate sales or in which sales and interest rates are the only variables significant in investment decisions.[4] However, the essential point is that the rate of interest is one of those variables whose effect, whatever it may be, does tend to be an aggregative phenomenon and not, by its nature, a factor in which variations in experiences of one firm (such as a gain in sales at the expense of a competitor) are canceled substantially by similar changes in an opposite direction for another firm. The economic theorist is concerned precisely with those variables that help him explain the economy rather than with the particular actions of individual firms. Hence, it is not in itself decisive for economic theory that so many businessmen indicate that they do not consider the rate of interest in making investment decisions.[5]

More generally, the sophisticated investigator in this area must expect to find that the great bulk of explanations, descriptions, and rationalizations offered by his respondents are irrelevant to his model. This should cause no alarm and no rush to discard the model. It is exactly because it is a model and has the capacity to be useful as an explanatory device that it abstracts from the great body of data which, although perhaps significant to the individual businessman, are irrelevant to *its* purpose.

The foregoing should not be construed as meaning that models and theories must be impervious to interview and questionnaire findings. These findings can be very useful in enriching the model and offering links between empirical data and theoretical formulations which will make the latter more fruitful in empirical and substantive prediction. Thus, for example, statements by respondents that they do not consider the rate of interest but that they are seriously concerned with ratios of debt to equity and the effect of new stock issues upon the price

---

[4] In the real world, changes in aggregate sales are certainly, in the opinion of this writer, a major determinant of the aggregate of investment. The issue of methodological propriety in establishing this point is hence all the more important.

[5] An understanding of marginal concepts is significant in this instance. Investment expenditures tend, for the individual firm, to represent discrete, "lumpy" projects. In only a small proportion of such projects would it be reasonable to expect profitability to be at the margin of acceptability, where a variation in interest costs would prove significant. The general point involved here is treated at greater length in a comment by the writer in *Studies in Income and Wealth*, XVII, 484-88.

of existing securities may suggest for empirical testing and fitting into our theoretical formulation certain variables which are actually importantly related to interest rates, money markets, and/or cost of capital in general. On the other hand, complaints of difficulties in securing credit from banks may be more basically related to other variables, such as profit prospects, than to the availability of capital itself. Thus a firm with uncertain sales and profits prospects might well have difficulty financing a contemplated capital expenditure and might ascribe to availability of funds the role of investment inhibitor. Yet in this case the banks or capital markets would merely be reacting to other variables which the economist might more properly consider relevant.

Above all, the investigator must avoid what may be called a public opinion poll mentality which would decide issues of economic theory by a meaningless majority vote. Much of our theory relates to marginal considerations. The traditional role of the interest rate in influencing the level of investment may be quite consistent with a situation in which only 5 percent of firms pay any attention to the interest rate. Ubiquitous rules of thumb by which businessmen appear to operate in 90 percent of the cases reveal highly significant information in the 10 percent which are exceptions. And businessmen's descriptions, rationalizations, and explanations of what they do may enable us to complement economic theory; they are certainly no substitute for economic theory.

II. SCOPE AND METHOD OF THE STUDY

In the spring of 1950 a series of interviews of a pilot nature were conducted by Franco Modigliani and members of the staff of the Merrill Foundation project in "Expectations and Business Fluctuations." These involved almost exclusively firms in the agricultural equipment industry and emphasized problems of capital expenditures and forward planning. This work was carried forward by the present writer through interviews with officials of 14 manufacturing corporations in the Midwest and East in the winter and spring of 1951-52.[6] In a number of cases reinterviews were undertaken in 1954 and 1955.

The industries selected were agricultural equipment, shoe manufacturing, beer, containers (paper and cardboard), steel, and rubber. The firms included were generally extremely large, with annual sales in several cases exceeding one billion dollars, and were typically the largest or among the largest in their industry. Interviewees ranged from presidents, board chairmen, and executive vice-presidents to controllers, treasurers, production schedulers, and firm economists. Most firms were visited several times, with interviews generally commencing with a top executive and then continuing with various subordinate officers. In the course of the interviews, firm documents and statistics were solicited, and where obtained, have been studied and are being subjected to a continuing analysis.

The firms selected can in no sense be considered either random or representative samples of American industry as a whole. Indeed, the entire work may be considered largely in the nature of a pilot study with findings and conclusions all put forward explicitly for purposes of independent verification. However, it may be claimed that the firms covered represent in themselves such substantial portions of important industries that results achieved may be of more than passing interest.[7]

Interviews were relatively unstructured, with no formal, written schedule of questions. However, the interviewer was generally able to

---

[6] Initial contact was made by a letter sent out over the signature of the Dean of the College of Commerce of the University of Illinois, explaining briefly the nature of the project and introducing the interviewer. The latter then took over the correspondence and generally received very substantial cooperation from the firms concerned.

[7] Coverage reflected in part the desire to include both industries engaged primarily in consumer goods production and those with large or dominant interests in the production of capital goods. Another criterion in industry selection was location. Of the industries included, all or at least a number of the major firms had central offices in the Midwest. Top management of all but one of the firms included were located in Illinois, Missouri, or Ohio

take copious notes which make possible fairly accurate direct quotations of interviewees. To make available exact written remarks reflecting in some cases more careful thought on the matters raised, terminal letters were addressed to top officials previously interviewed, both in the 14 firms visited and in those included in the earlier pilot study, asking summary questions relating to the issues under consideration. Finally, drafts of the general material of this paper as well as the reports on their own firms were sent to each of the companies studied, with requests for comments, corrections, and answers to various specific questions that seemed to require clarification.

It should be understood that a substantial portion of the interviewing efforts was directed to acquisition of information bearing on the formation and influence of entrepreneurial expectations. The interviews described herein were but one phase of the major research in "Expectations and Business Fluctuations," under the over-all direction of Professor Modigliani. The interviews were thus directed explicitly toward complementation of various associated theoretical and empirical investigations. For example, specific attention was given to the nature of estimates of capital expenditures furnished to surveyors in connection with Jean Bronfenbrenner Crockett's work on Department of Commerce-Securities and Exchange Commission anticipations-realization data.[8] The formation of sales expectations and their reflection both in capital expenditure plans and in production scheduling were examined carefully in the light of developing hypotheses by Modigliani and Owen H. Sauerlender[9] and by Robert Ferber,[10] whose findings point to the regressive, "conservative" character of expectations. And information on capital expenditure plans was solicited with a particular view of contributing to the hypotheses set forth by Modigliani in relation to the planning horizon.[11] Though leading to some attention to matters which are peripheral to this paper, this role in the "expectations" project did involve a major focus on capital expenditures and on production planning and inventory control, both of which are of course integrally related to anticipations of future conditions affecting the firm.

---

[8] See Irwin Friend and Jean Bronfenbrenner, "Plant and Equipment Programs and their Realization," *Studies in Income and Wealth*, XVII, 53-98.

[9] "Economic Expectations and Plans of Firms in Relation to Short-Term Forecasting," presented at the National Bureau conference on short-term forecasting at Ann Arbor, Michigan, in 1951, published in revised form in *Studies in Income and Wealth*, XVII, 261-351.

[10] *The Railroad Shippers' Forecasts* (Urbana: University of Illinois, Bureau of Economic and Business Research, 1953).

[11] Abstract in *Econometrica*, XX, No 3 (July, 1952), 481-2.

In regard to capital expenditures, the interviewer was hunting in general for determinants of the level of expenditures. This involved the examination of (1) the effective lines of authority for proposing, accepting, and rejecting various types of expenditures; (2) the extent to which well-defined criteria exist for accepting or rejecting specific expenditures, the nature of these criteria, and the degree to which they vary in accordance with the type of capital expenditure (such as replacement, expansion, or new products, or small versus large outlays); (3) the influence of cost of capital and availability of internal funds, of long-run extrapolations of current trend versus assumptions that current rates will be maintained, of explicit or implicit allowances for uncertainty, the time dimension of capital expenditure plans, changes, and execution; (4) the extent to which factors other than profitability play a role in investment decisions; and (5) some indications of the nature of data on capital expenditures and capital expenditure plans which would be obtained from questionnaire surveys.

The conclusions offered in the following pages should be checked against the interview data from which they have been derived. For the interview technique is by its nature a very personal method of research and one's fellow economists in instances like this have every right to wonder whether they have anything more as a reporter of interviews than, at best, a good storyteller. There may, unfortunately, be as many only vaguely related "stories" as there are tellers. "Morals" of the stories are likely to be at least as numerous. An effort has been made, therefore, by means of fairly extensive quotations and presentation of material on a firm-by-firm basis in the context in which it was gathered, to bring the reader as close to the original data of this study as appears reasonably feasible. By the nature of an interview study, this degree of closeness to the data cannot be very great. Nevertheless, the reader is encouraged to utilize the more detailed firm-by-firm presentations to go beyond — and back over — the writer's own analysis and conclusions. Further, these, like all other interview findings, should be subjected to rigorous criticism and the attempt of verification by means of other techniques of analysis.

III. ANALYSIS OF FINDINGS[12]

A dominant characteristic of most of the firms studied was growth. Many of the firms had completed major post-World-War-II expansions. Most had benefited from direct government contracts or the indirect effects upon aggregate demand stemming from the Korean War, which was in progress at the time of the initial interviews. All were in industries that have been characterized by a long-term upward trend in output and sales.

It may be argued, as a consequence, that our findings will emphasize disproportionately the role of expansion and long-run growth factors as determinants of capital expenditures. Such an argument, however, may turn out to be ill-grounded. For one thing, most American firms have exhibited similar characteristics of growth; those firms and industries which have not have been the exceptions. Secondly, it is certainly the growing industries which have accounted for the bulk of the economy's capital expenditures. What explains capital expenditures in these growing firms and industries must perforce go far toward the explanation of aggregate expenditures.

In spite of this general context of growth, the 1949-50 recession had had sufficient impact for questions relating to behavior in a period of cyclical downturn to appear meaningful to most of the interviewees. To what extent responses conditioned by the 1949-50 experience may be useful in predicting behavior in the face of a deeper and longer-term drop is uncertain.

Nature and Extent of Forward Estimates and Capital Expenditure Plans

Capital expenditures beyond trivial amounts are not entered into lightly. Rather they are treated as matters of great importance requiring consideration by the highest levels of management. Most characteristically they are tied to basic, long-run evaluations of the economic situation affecting the firm.

Most firms made some effort to ascertain long-term trends in demand. In the rubber and tire industry, in particular, there was a well-organized system of forecasts by each company of industry demand, the forecasts being pooled, reported, and averaged at periodic meetings of the Rubber Manufacturers Association. These industry forecasts are

---

[12] This section is a considerably expanded and modified version of the summary analysis of these data appearing in "Interview and Other Survey Techniques and the Study of Investment," *Studies in Income and Wealth,* Vol XIX.

generally available and might offer an interesting field for statistical analysis. However, they are merely elements, not necessarily decisive, in the determination of expectations, and consequently, capital expenditures, of each individual firm. Indeed, forecasts of sales (or output) by the firm are closely guarded company secrets. And it is far from clear that top management was dominated by its own *staff* forecasts of the industry or economy.

In one agricultural equipment firm as well (Firm A),[13] there were found comparably elaborate forecasts of "normal demand" for the company's products in future years. In most cases, interviewees were proud to relate that they looked ahead and thought about the future. They were generally equally quick to discredit detailed forecasting.

If forward estimates are as precarious as was generally argued, why bother with them at all? Part of the answer is that they were not always bothered with. The extent of formal, statistical estimates of long-run demand was uneven. Some firms did more along this line than others. Some firms did more at one time — when major capital expenditures were under consideration — than at other times. One fairly general use of forward estimates of sales related to financial planning. Controllers, treasurers, and financial vice-presidents wished to know future sales receipts in order to plan acquisition of the additional funds that might be required to finance future output. Financing problems tended to loom larger when firms were committing themselves to heavy capital expenditures. In addition, forward sales estimates of a long-run nature were frequently justified by their role in capital expenditure decisions.

Capital expenditure plans generally extended less far into the future than the long-range demand forecasts to which they were tied. This can of course be explained in terms of the general notion that today's capital expenditures must be justified by sales in tomorrow's tomorrows. Capital expenditure plans frequently tapered off as they went forward. The first year ahead might involve plans of expenditures by quarters; figures for subsequent periods were listed on an annual basis. Moreover, there was a tendency to list known future expenditures only, so that as one got into the unknown future the volume of planned expenditures shrank.

There were various evidences of thinking oriented to the problem of an uncertain future. Thus, one agricultural equipment firm (Firm A)

---

[13] Identifications in parentheses refer to the individual firm reports in Chapter IV.

referred to "possible market situations" to explain "Projects Requiring Further Study (And Not Provided For In Present Financial Program)." A large steel company (Firm C) indicated that of a large volume of expenditures "in mind" but not in a plan perhaps only a fourth were realized. A container company (Firm H) cited "iffies" which might or might not materialize. A shoe manufacturing firm (Firm J) gave detailed evidence of the cautious step-by-step manner in which major expenditures were conceived, planned, and executed.

Since most firms evidenced few illusions about their ability to predict the details of future developments — or even predict accurately their broad outlines — they attempted to set up strategies for future action, committing themselves only as far ahead as was necessary. In a number of cases, land might be purchased in various localities to permit building new plants where, when, and if appropriate. Or new processes might be tried first in one plant, with their introduction in other plants contingent upon later developments.[14]

Yet the extent and significance of forward planning of capital expenditures were minimized by many, if not most, respondents. Thus, a relatively smaller steel company (Firm D) emphasized that capital expenditure plans were not formal and that the firm was not enthusiastic about *long-run* planning. A regional brewery (Firm F) explained that major items were foreseen but there was no real plan for other expenditures. A large container company (Firm G) denied the use of long-run budgets or forecasts. One shoe company (Firm J) reported no long-run capital expenditure plans and another (Firm I) reported taking "each case as it comes." One rubber and tire company (Firm L) indicated specifically that long-run demand forecasts were necessary for capital expenditures but that the firm had no long-run capital expenditure plans. Another rubber and tire company (Firm M) emphasized

---

[14] Note the correspondence of these findings with the formulation by Modigliani (*Econometrica*, July, 1952, p. 482):

". . . When we recognize the cost of forming expectations and of planning, and take into account the fact that information on events expected for a given point of time is likely to increase at no cost as that point approaches, we may expect to find that the relevant expectation and planning horizon involves a subset, possibly a small subset of all future parameters and moves.

"Since only the first move can be implemented, no other future move need be planned explicitly even if it is 'relevant.' However, as relevant moves appear in the system that has to be solved in order to decide the first move, they may be explicitly planned as a by-product of the solution for the first move. But these plans are not final decisions about later moves; such decisions will be reached at the proper time on the basis of information that will be available at that time . . ."

that there was only a limited amount of *formal* forward planning of capital expenditures.

One should perhaps caution against accepting at face value the frequent assertions by financial officers and others in top management echelons with final responsibility for capital expenditure decisions that there are no capital expenditures beyond the approved budget. For such statements may reflect to a large degree a sort of intra-firm discipline designed to prevent subordinate officials from acting as if they have a claim on the future funds of the firm. Hence it may not rule out the existence of at least implicit or informal longer-range plans guiding the firm's actions. Yet one should also note that what may frequently (particularly in questionnaire surveys) pass as capital expenditure plans are really estimates or predictions by the controller. As such, they have the property of expectations or anticipations rather than plans or commitments which the firm can be expected to implement.

A substantial amount of this de-emphasis on long-run capital expenditure plans may relate to the period of this study. Many firms were completing or had completed major expansion programs which had been planned earlier. Completion of these programs left the firms without the necessity, for a while, of long-run planning. This would suggest that the extent as well as the seriousness and formal character of long-run plans is not constant. Expenditures are planned well in advance when there is some reason to do so, but not as a matter of general principle to be observed on all occasions. Many firms planned ahead five years in their major postwar expansions but revealed briefer planning periods when major expansions were completed. It may be inferred that the length of forward capital expenditure plans varies with the amount of the capital expenditure program. This phenomenon may reflect an awareness of the effects of U-shaped supply curves of materials, capital, and the services of management or "entrepreneurship" itself, which would necessitate planning to achieve a judicious spreading of expenditures over time.

One way of explaining the caution with which the firms interviewed appear to make commitments pertaining to current capital expenditures as well as their apparently low estimate of the utility of long-run plans would be to state that they have a relatively high discount for risk and uncertainty. Since the distant future is more uncertain than the near future, expectations with regard to the relatively near future are likely to prove decisive. As firms delay expenditures designed to pay off in some future period, expectations with regard to that period require less discounting for uncertainty and hence assume sufficient weight to justify consideration. This approach may, of course, help explain the tendency for capital expenditures, even on projects which must pay off over a period considerably longer than that of the business cycle, to be made in periods of prosperity. Proper attention to the implicit value of the businessman's high rate of discount for risk and uncertainty may, by the way, enable one to defend more easily the hypothesis that the actions of firms may be viewed as if they are essentially rational. For firms may have good reason to discount highly data which loom large to the outside investigator. Admittedly, though, the rationality may not always be obvious to one unfamiliar with the preference functions of the management of the firm — and the personnel of that management may be incapable of articulating the essential, implicit rationality of their actions.

However, against this risk factor, shortening the horizon, must be set the necessity for long-lived assets to be paying propositions over a long period, which probably tends, on balance, to make firms relatively resistant to short-term fluctuations. To the extent that they are, they may offer an interesting confirmation of the instability hypothesis offered by the French economist, Aftalion, many years ago, which likens the economy to a cold room with a fireplace which is slow to heat up. The reluctance of management to react capriciously to momentary changes may make them ignore developing signs of disaster during a prosperous period. They thus invest too long during the heated boom, and, through a refusal to believe the first indications of upswing, delay investment too long after the chilling crisis-depression catharsis.

Formal Aspects of Approval

There is little that may be offered in the way of generalizations on the details of procedures by which the various firms formulate and decide upon capital expenditures. What little is offered may appear particularly lacking in distinction from earlier contributions by others who have approached business firms to find out *how* business decisions are made.[15]

It may be noted briefly that projects appear to emanate both from top management and from operating and engineering departments. General expansion expenditures tend to originate with top management. Particu-

---

[15] The reader interested in more detailed information on this score, however, may be referred to the recent National Industrial Conference Board report on *Controlling Capital Expenditures* (Studies in Business Policy, No. 62, New York, 1953), as well as to the analyses of interviews of the current study.

lar cost reductions or technological economies may stem from engineers and operating people. Although major expenditures generally require approval by the board of directors, they are usually thrashed out informally before they reach the board so that formal rejections appear to be relatively rare. Individual smaller expenditures are frequently approved merely by operating people or single officials out of blanket authorizations which are agreed upon by the board of directors (or some such top group). There is apparent also a certain tendency for top management to screen and reduce the amount of requests which have come up from below, or to set up criteria which will reduce the number of expenditure requests coming up. In the words of the president of a large container firm (Firm G), "We constantly have much more submitted from our people down the line than either the management committee or the board of directors approves." In spite of the substantial evidence of requests for specific expenditures originating from general managers, department heads, engineers, and others below the top levels of management, it seems clear that with final approval resting with top management and with the criteria for both submission of requests and their approval set by top management, there is a high degree of centralization of the determinants of capital expenditure decisions.

However centralized the final responsibility and authority, one must observe differences of opinion or at least of emphasis within the firm. Different departments tend to operate as a rough system of checks and balances, reflecting the partially independent functions and sometimes divergent immediate goals of various specific elements in the organization.

In a number of firms, procedures for requesting capital expenditures involve the categorization of each proposed expenditure, with criteria and channels of approval dependent upon both the category and the amount. The categories and the corresponding criteria are intended to offer ready operating rules for those whose duties involve initiating, evaluating, or passing upon requests for capital expenditures. The classifications indicate, in some cases by their nature and in some cases with accompanying instructions, the scope and substance of required profit or cost-saving estimates and calculations. Some of the sets of categories are as follows:

maintenance, repair, expansion, savings;
diversification of product, improvement of quality, obsolescence, increase of capacity;
replacement, expansion;
replacement, economies, expansion, new products.

Maintenance, repair, and replacement categories generally require no profitability calculations. Gains accounted for under "savings" or "obsolescence" must usually be calculated under the assumption of current volume of operations. Somewhere along the line expansion projects run into the question of "for how long?" If the need for expansion appears temporary or uncertain, it is likely that favorable consideration will be given to one or several of various alternatives to the purchase or construction of new capital assets. Such alternatives might involve increasing employment of labor, utilizing outside suppliers, revamping old plants or reactivating idle ones, or simply sacrificing sales (possibly with favorable price results).

However, the overlapping of categories is generally recognized. Although this overlapping is frequently cited by business respondents, it probably occurs in equally numerous and important instances (important from the standpoint of economic analysts, not necessarily from the standpoint of the businessman) in which business respondents do not call attention to it. Thus the interviewer-analyst may note that businessmen see an increase in demand as forcing the working of high-cost extra shifts and the development of costly bottlenecks. Yet certain laborsaving devices or expenditures designed to ease bottlenecks would be classified as cost reducing, i.e., justifiable in terms of savings. Should they be considered so by the analyst or should they be considered instead as devices for rightward movement of a U-shaped cost curve, on the rising part of which the firm may be operating, thus lowering costs per unit for the current output, *and* permitting expansion of output at current costs?

The Role of Expansion

A major determinant of capital expenditures, as revealed by the interviews, is the need for additional capacity to meet increases in demand. Emphasis, however, is on long-run rather than on short-run changes in demand. And in a number of cases the pressure of increased demand on capacity is expressed in terms of rising costs, so that capital expenditures which are made fundamentally in response to rising demand are reported as ostensibly for purposes of cost reduction.

Thus, in one farm equipment firm (Firm A), it was pointed out that a shortage of capacity reflected itself in higher-cost, multi-shift operation. The decision to increase plant was a function of bottlenecks (discontinuities or vertical portions in the marginal cost curve), alternate requirements for funds, alternate methods of expansion (longer hours, additional shifts, use of more outside suppliers), and the confidence of expectations that increased capacity would prove justified over a sufficiently long period. In a second farm equipment firm (Firm B), it was emphasized that there was a reluctance to meet temporary shortages of capacity. Since it took two years to provide a permanent increase in capacity the company would rather make temporary provisions than permanently expand plant unless a current trend of increased demand could be expected to continue. In both agricultural equipment firms it was indicated that provision for some (high) average level of demand rather than exceptional peaks was the aim in planning capacity.

Similarly, in a large integrated steel company (Firm C), we learn that the firm is interested in the long run, not in temporary movements. Major capital expenditures are again those related to expansion. However, one interesting note relating capital expenditures to general conditions rather than to the particular demand for output of the firm may be seen in the incentive to the company to create new iron capacity when a generally high demand in the industry induces scrap shortages which raise the price of scrap iron. In a smaller steel products firm (Firm D), the possibility of a seven-day week as an alternative to permanent expansion was raised again. A container company (Firm H) pointed out that it will revamp one of its old plants, whenever possible, before acquiring a new one. This company also cited the possibility of capital expenditures that will permit production by the firm of material previously obtained from outside suppliers. Here again, general economic conditions will impinge sharply on the supply situation for the individual firm.

In the shoe industry also there was an emphasis on the importance of distinguishing between temporary fads and long-run changes in sales, in spite of the competitive pressure to react rapidly to style changes and new developments in consumer demand. Again, in the rubber and tire industry, which is dominated by the history and prospect of major growth, it was indicated that expansion would not be undertaken for minor increases in demand. Here, as elsewhere, the possibility of acquisition of existing assets — in the form of government-owned plants — suggested an additional caution against careless application of information on determinants of capital expenditures of the individual firm to the problem of aggregate investment.

The role of changes in demand as a determinant of capital expenditures is revealed implicitly in a number of instances where what appear to be other factors are mentioned explicitly. Thus, in one rubber and tire company (Firm N), preserving its place in the industry was cited as a motive for capital expenditures. But this can be explained as meaning that when demand for tires (for example) increases with output already near capacity levels, capital expenditures are necessary for a firm to capture its share of the increased demand. It is the increase in demand which induces the investment. Preservation of place in the industry is perhaps in part a rule of thumb for keeping up with long-run changes in demand. A similar note was struck by the controller of a farm equipment company (Firm B), who declared, "If our share were falling in a capacity market we would expand. If our share were falling in a falling or stationary market we might cut prices." The former situation is one in which production is proceeding at a capacity rate and the fall in market share is occasioned by the firm's inability to meet demand, coupled with a greater ability by other firms in the industry to meet this demand (or at least their own traditional share of the demand, with some of the demand for the industry's products then being lost to the entire industry). The share-of-the-market factor can thus be interpreted as meaning that a firm would expand to meet an increase in demand if the alternative were a permanent sacrifice of sales rather than a mere deferral to a future slack period. The rule of thumb for determining a permanent sacrifice of sales in a "capacity market" is a falling share in that market.

In a number of cases investment was brought about by moves into new products or moves to new locations. But the new products frequently constituted additions to the demand for already existing products and the new locations, as in the case of container plants and breweries, involved expansion to meet demand in new areas in addition to the already existing demand in old areas.

On the other hand, it is conceivable that a substantial amount of capacity-increasing capital expenditures may be viewed as cost reducing in purpose. To the extent that a firm is moved by increasing demand to the rising portion of a U-shaped short-run cost curve,[16] new plant and equipment, by putting the firm on lower portions of new short-run cost curves to the right of the old curves, may be viewed as lowering average cost at existing outputs or as increasing capacity at existing costs.

The tie-in between cost-reducing and capacity-expanding factors

---

[16] Or, more generally, merely to the right of the point of tangency between the short-run and long-run average cost curves, whether they are falling, level, or rising at that point.

in investment can be variously illustrated. For one thing, numerous executives stated directly that modernizing improvements and replacements increase capacity. Beer companies explained that they reduced shipping costs by setting up additional plants in new areas in which sales had developed. In steel, when demand is high, increased costs of scrap may induce construction of basic steel facilities, which would reduce the cost of iron to the company and increase its availability in the industry. Improvements in equipment can, as suggested by one rubber firm (Firm M), tend to reduce expenditures necessary for expanded plant facilities by permitting more economical plant layouts in new plants.

In terms of current economic theory, then, there is much in the interview material which may be used to confirm the acceleration principle. However, such confirmation would not be on the crude level which would have current investment a unique function of changes in demand in a specific (generally immediately) past period. Rather, a suggestion as to the difficulties in the way of statistical confirmation of the acceleration principle, particularly at the level of aggregates, may be found in evidences of entrepreneurial caution, lengthy lags in response, and peculiarities in supply functions. Hence, the generalized Hicksian *Trade Cycle* model with a variety of lags may prove more useful than the simple second-order difference equation presented by Samuelson in his well-known multiplier-accelerator article.[17] And of course, indications in this study of a lagged but pervasive influence of expansion upon investment fit easily into growth models such as those of Harrod,[18] Domar,[19] and others.

---

[17] Paul A. Samuelson, "Interactions between the Multiplier Analysis and the Principle of Acceleration," *Review of Economic Statistics*, XXI (1939), 75 ff.

[18] See R. F. Harrod, "An Essay in Dynamic Theory," *Economic Journal*, March, 1939, as reprinted in Harrod's *Economic Essays* (New York: Harcourt, Brace and Company, 1953), p. 269, and "Supplement on Dynamic Theory," *ibid.*, p. 278. Harrod maintains that changes in sales operate to increase *ex ante* investment. The existence of backlogs of demand for plant and equipment inhibits the adjustment of *ex post* investment. However, the resultant discrepancy between *ex ante* and *ex post* investment, while making empirical confirmation of the acceleration principle difficult, leaves change of sales with a major influence on the course of investment and economic activities.

[19] See Evsey D. Domar, "The Problem of Capital Accumulation," *American Economic Review*, XXXVIII, No. 5 (December, 1948), pp. 777-94. The importance of Domar's central problem, the dependence of a high rate of investment on a *growing* national income, receives substantial confirmation in our emphasis on the role of expansion in capital expenditures.

The Roles of Nonexpansionary Expenditures and of Replacement

At least one notion from which have been drawn conclusions with serious policy implications may be called into question by our findings. This relates to the assumption that we may rely upon a high volume of capital expenditures being substantially sustained by expenditures labeled for "replacement" and "modernization" or for other purposes separate from expansion. It appears rather that such "replacement" and "modernization" expenditures are actually subject to many if not most of the economic vicissitudes which have caused major fluctuations in capital expenditures which are explicitly for purposes of expansion. Similarly, despite evidence of rules of thumb which tend to allow expenditure of depreciation allowances for "replacement," it is not clear that high depreciation charges can be relied upon to maintain a high level of replacement expenditures. In the last analysis most expenditures seem subject to tests of profitability which offer no ground for expecting stability in the firm's expenditures in a world of fluctuation. The rules and formulas are changed where appropriate.

There are, however, data which might help explain the weakness, observed frequently in statistical analysis, of relations between the rate of capital expenditures and changes in demand. In an interview occurring early in 1952, the controller of an agricultural equipment firm (Firm B) declared: "We are replacing when things fall apart. If replacement is planned, when replacement comes along the 'replaced' asset and its replacement are both used." Commenting more than two years later, a high executive of this firm explained in correspondence that this statement had reflected a particular circumstance of the time of the interview, and not a general policy:

In 1952, we were in the midst of a combination of circumstances entailing (1) pent-up demand in excess of productive capacity, and (2) long delays in procurement of new capital tools and equipment. At the same time, government preference for our products was forcing good commercial customers into our competitors. More output was, accordingly, most essential — and for the time being was more important than the lower unit costs which could be attained if obsolescent equipment could be replaced by modern machinery. It was not that we did not wish to make replacements. We couldn't. Whatever new capital equipment we could get was applied to *more* output on top of what we could get from continued use of old equipment.

This would indicate that the designation of capital expenditures for expansion or replacement would itself depend upon the level of demand or output. For at high levels of output retirements would be postponed and expenditures which might otherwise be justified as buying replacements would actually be adding to existing equipment. On the other hand, at lower levels of output the same expenditures might be justified as replacing high-cost equipment which, in view of the level of activity, it seemed appropriate to retire.

Regarding this from a slightly different analytical viewpoint, it may be said, as indicated earlier, that there is a tendency for the firm in a period of high output to move to the right on its *short-run* cost curve. Thus the firm does not buy as much new plant and equipment as it would if it were sure the new level of output would be maintained. Operation of the acceleration principle in the short run would be inhibited. Nevertheless, expenditures designated for "expansion" might appear large in periods of high and expanding output. This would be true because the upward slope of the cost curve at expanded outputs is so great that expenditure proposals which have the effect of lowering the cost curve as well as moving it to the right are now viewed primarily, as suggested before, as expanding capacity rather than reducing costs.

The interrelations of replacement, expansion, and economic conditions were further illustrated specifically in a number of firms. In another farm equipment firm (Firm A) it was clear that "replacement" involved improvement and expansion; replacement expenditures were related to the business cycle and managerial controls which offered no acyclical automaticity. A container company (Firm E) indicated that "replacement" permitted expansion. One rubber and tire company (Firm M) offered the information that replacement constituted improvement so that capacity could be expanded by merely investing depreciation allowances. Another rubber and tire company (Firm L) suggested that replacement expenditures were susceptible to an "economic reaction" and still another (Firm N) explained that "replacement expenditures," like most other expenditures, were postponable.

Price Considerations

It was indicated that construction costs are not a significant factor in determining the physical volume of investments. Higher costs must thus mean greater expenditures.

A major explanation of this apparently inelastic demand for capital goods is a widespread conviction among business executives that increased costs will be accompanied by increased product selling prices and increased earnings. One would therefore not be warranted in concluding that an increase in the *relative* prices of capital goods and other commodities would have little or no effect upon real investment.

One should note, too, that the significance of capital goods prices is implicitly a problem in marginalism where even near-unanimity of response may prove misleading. Major capital expenditures are frequently in the form of large integrated projects. If 90 percent of all firms interviewed had said that a 5-percent increase in construction costs had not led to any project cancellations but 10 percent had canceled their projects, the demand for investment goods as a whole might well be price-elastic.

Changing labor costs seem relevant to at least certain types of expenditures. They may induce expansion of facilities in new locations if changes in labor costs reveal locational or geographical differences. This was suggested by a shoe firm (Firm J) and seemed to receive corroboration in the interviews with one agricultural equipment firm (Firm A).

Supply of Money Capital

The interviews suggested that the supply of money capital was not a crucial determinant of capital expenditures. "We'll get the money if we need it" was a common refrain. Yet there was repeated evidence that the problem of obtaining funds was an important one in at least the financial departments of the firm. Conclusions drawn from the remarks of various of the controllers interviewed might even indicate (misleadingly) that availability of funds must be a decisive factor in investment decisions.

While not allowing oneself to be influenced unduly by the remarks of those who may emphasize financial considerations because of their own preoccupations, one must likewise be careful not to be misled by those who ignore financial considerations because these are not *their* particular concern. Thus a production man who must justify proposed capital expenditures in terms of whether they promise increased profits or cost savings sufficient to meet some specified earnings criteria may easily respond that it is not the cost or availability of capital that concerns him but only the expected profitability (or cost saving). Yet the parameters of the earnings criteria which the production man accepts as given may themselves be determined by the availability and/or cost of capital.

Questions directed at the role of "the interest rate" received almost uniformly negative response. However, by "the interest rate" the business respondent hardly conceives of the symbol of a whole structure of capital costs to which the theoretical economist has given so much attention. Our interviews suggest the need for fewer stereotyped questions in this area and more careful probing along lines of concepts of capital cost which seem relevant to the firm. This might lead to problems such as ascertaining constraints as to debt-equity ratios and analyzing the effects of interest rates and the floating of new stock on existing corporate securities.

The need for care in investigating is shown too by consideration of the problem of availability of funds. It was reported by one brewery (Firm F) that elaborate earnings calculations had been undertaken to convince the bankers of the desirability of a loan. In at least this interview, then, it became quite clear that availability of funds was hardly a variable exogenous to the economic prospects of the firm.

By way of substantiating these various points we may call attention to the following further bits of evidence in the interviews.

One farm equipment company (Firm A) thinks explicitly of cost of capital in terms of a composite of the costs of money acquired through common stock (where the cost was calculated as the ratio of earnings to the market value of stock), preferred stock, borrowing, and liabilities (which would be counted as "no cost").

A vice-president of another farm equipment company (Firm B) declared that the "responsibility for *not* approving management-recommended investment could often be greater than responsibility for approval." In other words, one should keep in mind the expected return from investment, and not be dominated by the cost.

A top officer in a large steel company (Firm C), in explaining the criteria for optimum debt structures, indicated the operation of cost-of-capital considerations in terms of "dilution of stock" and debt-equity ratios, but it seemed clear that these considerations did not offer absolute constraints with regard to capital expenditures.

The controller of a national brewery (Firm E) revealed that in spite of the desire to minimize costs, there were times when an expansion program had to proceed even though the cost of financing was higher than expected.

The president of a container company (Firm H) stated clearly that lack of funds or the necessity of borrowing did not and would not restrain the company from expansion. The president of a shoe company (Firm I) said, "We're not influenced by the cost of money. We won't put in a new plant unless demand warrants it."

The financial vice-president of a rubber and tire company (Firm L) declared, "We have not had to be influenced by availability of funds on capital expenditure, plans in domestic business." He did explain, however, his concern for getting whatever funds proved necessary on the most advantageous terms possible.

Taxes

Interviews suggested the merit of further attention to the operation of the various phenomena of capital formation under the substantial influence of current tax and tax-related regulations. Thus the effect of the excess profits tax, if testimony from several firms is to be given credence, was not merely to reduce the net cost of interest but to make it negative. Also, the effect of ordinary profits taxes is not simply, as some investigators have been inclined to report, to reduce capital expenditures by reducing the amount of funds available. For high taxes on profits also appear to induce certain expenditures which can be added to current costs and thus reduce current tax liabilities. Such expenditures might be desirable if they were expected to yield increased profits in the future, when tax rates might be lower, or merely yield utility of some other nontaxable kind, such as greater security for the firm. In the context of high corporate profits and excess profits tax rates, the accelerated amortization rights granted under government "certificates of necessity" were reported by some firms to have had a substantial effect in the direction of increasing capital expenditures.[20]

Calculations

Consideration of the various formal costs and earnings criteria reportedly used by business firms in deciding upon capital expenditures led into something of a wilderness where method was difficult to find. Rules of thumb appeared unduly crude and frequently internally inconsistent. Under probing questioning, responsible officials indicated ignorance as to the specific nature of the calculations underlying their rules or they advised sagely that "judgment" was more important than rules.

Most firms reported some kind of pay-off criterion for capital ex-

---

[20] See the discussion on pp. 16-18 of the fallacy of composition which may be involved in interpreting interview comments on accelerated amortization It might also be pointed out that accelerated amortization privileges are likely to bulk much larger in business minds in periods of high profits and high taxes than during the depths of the depression, when profits and profits taxes tend to be nil.

penditures. In one case a two-year pay-off was described as an automatic qualification, in another case three years; but more generally, passing of such a hurdle would merely qualify a proposed expenditure for consideration at the appropriate higher management level. Pay-offs seemed more relevant for proposed equipment than for plant. This may in part explain the relatively short length of the pay-off period, since equipment is likely to be relatively short-lived. The short length was also explained by recognition of the need to discount for future technological change and obsolescence.

Expected earnings or savings, expressed as a percentage of the proposed expenditure, were used fairly frequently, at least to provide a cutoff point below which capital expenditures should not be proposed. There was some evidence of companies desiring, although not necessarily requiring, that new investment offer a return equal to the existing earnings rate calculated on the firm's net worth. In other cases (Firm N, in particular) various (and varying) rates were set depending upon the category of proposed capital expenditures. It was clear, however, that there were almost always large numbers of expenditures that were not susceptible to pay-off or earnings calculations. In addition, major expenditures such as those involved in large expansion programs were apparently predicated on management judgment much more than on the accountant's calculations.

The prevalence of formulas which involve annual operating profits and ignore prospective life of assets is frequently perplexing, if not exasperating. Similarly, the handling of depreciation charges in these formulas is downright offensive to one nurtured in the concepts of the marginal efficiency of investment. In some cases, for example, the crudities of calculations and criteria for capital expenditures appear to lend a distinct bias in favor of short-lived assets. But then one may observe differential standards of a nature that appear likely to compensate for the "errors" one sees in the businessman's measures. Thus, much of the "bias" in favor of short-lived assets may involve merely a greater rate of discount for risk and uncertainty, as suggested earlier, and a sharper time preference than the outside investigator may be reckoning with.

To the extent that information was obtained about calculation procedures, it was found that they generally involved estimates of earnings or cost savings on an annual basis. No allowance was made for the number of years over which earnings might be received or cost savings realized. (In the case of investments which were not expected to show immediate returns or savings, estimates might be made for some year in the future rather than for the period immediately following the expenditure, but again it was the *annual* return and not the *sum* of returns which entered into the calculations.) Depreciation charges were made against the incomes expected from the prospective capital additions. Where prospective additions were being compared with existing properties which they were to replace, depreciation charges were also made against the old properties (unless they were already completely written off) in estimating comparative costs.

Typical business calculations of savings, earnings, or profit ratios, whatever their ultimate rationale, are theoretically crude and do involve mathematical inconsistencies. Generally, for example, depreciation allowances are deducted from the flow of savings but not from the capital costs with which these savings are compared. This, with the use of estimates for a single year, which involves the failure to include the discounted sum of future returns, results in a general underestimate of true expected rates of profit and in a rather complex bias in regard to assets of various durabilities.[21]

It can be verified that, within relevant ranges of the variables, the method of calculation indicated above underestimates the true rate of profit or yield, based on consistent discounting, for virtually all projected capital additions. (Only properties to last one year, which would be charged to expense anyway, and properties to last forever, which would have no charges for depreciation, would show yields by the described method which were equal to the true rate of profit. In all other cases the calculated yields would underestimate the true rate.) For example, equipment with an expected life of 5 years and an apparent profit rate of 10 percent entails a true profit rate of some 15 percent. Similarly, plant expected to last 30 years with an apparent profit rate of 10 percent would have a true rate of profit of 13 percent.[22] To the extent that appropriate decision makers do not, explicitly

---

[21] The calculations analyzed here are essentially similar to those described by Michael Gort in "The Planning of Investment: A Study of Capital Budgeting in the Electric Power Industry," *Journal of Business*, XXIV (July, 1951), especially pages 193-96. The analysis in this study is virtually identical with the analysis of the calculations described by Gort and of those of rubber and tire Firm N offered in "Interview and Other Survey Techniques and the Study of Investment," *Studies in Income and Wealth*, Vol XIX.

[22] These figures and the following table are calculated from the formulation in footnote 23 relating the true expected rate of profit, $\frac{1}{r} - 1$, to the firm's definition of expected profit, p, and the expected earning life of the property, n.

(*Footnote concluded on next page*)

or implicitly, allow for this underestimate (for example, in comparing the expected profit rate with *ex post* earnings on previously invested capital), the underestimate of expected profit rates may tend to discourage capital expenditures generally. To the extent, however, that these calculations are merely empirical rules of thumb of an ordinal nature for screening and ranking proposed capital expenditures, one may presume that the acceptable cutoff point reflects the average true rate of profit desired by a firm on new investment, regardless of the nominal rate indicated by the calculations. Without necessarily (or probably) knowing precisely why, a firm wishing to raise its *ex post* profits on capital in the future over some present figure, say 12 percent, might thus be moved to lower its nominal profit requirement to 10 percent (or less). For it would discover by experience that where expectations were realized, expenditures promising 10 percent did actually tend to raise *ex post* profits above 12 percent.

It may be demonstrated also that assets with given apparent profit ratios reveal a true rate of profit which is lowest for properties expected to last either one year or forever (assuming straight-line de-

$\frac{1}{r} - 1$ ("True rate of profit")

n	p = 10%	p = 25%	p = 30%	p = 50%
1	10.0%	25.0%	30.0%	50.0%
2	13.1	31.9	38.4	61.8
3	14.4	34.2	40.5	64.7
4	15.0	34.9	41.1	64.8
5	15.2	34.9	41.0	64.1
6	15.3	34.7	40.6	63.1
7	15.4	34.3	40.0	62.0
8	15.3	33.9	39.5	61.1
9	15.2	33.4	39.0	60.2
10	15.1	33.0	38.5	59.4
11	15.0	32.6	38.0	58.7
12	14.9	32.2	37.5	58.1
13	14.7	31.8	37.1	57.5
14	14.6	31.5	36.7	57.0
15	14.5	31.1	36.3	56.6
20	13.9	29.8	34.9	55.0
25	13.4	29.0	34.0	54.0
30	13.0	28.3	33.3	53.3
40	12.4	27.5	32.5	52.5
50	12.0	27.0	32.0	52.0
100	11.0	26.0	31.0	51.0
∞	10.0	25.0	30.0	50.0

preciation over the life of the property for all assets whose expected lives are one year or more). Maximum true rates of profit on invested capital are actually required by these calculations on properties whose expected lives are fairly short — in the neighborhood of five years.[23] It follows, of course, that for any given expected profit rate set by businessmen as necessary before a capital expenditure can be approved (or in many cases, even considered) by top management, the true rate of profit required is actually less if the proposed expenditure is for a long-term project or for an extremely short-term one. Since properties having extremely short lives are frequently charged to expense (not

---

[23] Let $p =$ the expected profit rate according to typical business calculations
Let $n =$ the number of years the asset will last.
Let $r =$ the rate of discount that will equate the sum of expected future returns to the present value of the asset
Assume, for simplicity, that the present or original value of the asset is unity.
Then the expected return must equal $\frac{1}{n} + p$, annually, for n years. But the real rate of return must involve discounting each annual return by r^t where t is the number of years which separates the date of the expected return from the present.

To solve for r we must set $1 = \left(\frac{1}{n}+p\right) \sum_{t=1}^{n} r^t$ (1)

whence $\dfrac{r(r^n - 1)}{r - 1} = \dfrac{1}{\frac{1}{n} + p}.$ (2)

It may then be observed that,

when $n = 1$, $r = \dfrac{1}{1+p}$, (3)

and as $n \to \infty$, $r \to \dfrac{1}{1+p}$. (4)

However, for reasonable values of p (where $0 < p < 1$), r reaches a minimum (and $\frac{1}{r} - 1$, the "true rate of profit," reaches a maximum) when $1 < n < \infty$; the exact value of n at which r is minimum depends upon the value given for p The value of $\frac{1}{r} - 1$ reaches its maximum for certain illustrative values of p at values of n, respectively, of about 7, 5, 4, and 4, as indicated in the following brief table

(1) Apparent rate of profit p	(2) Value of n which maximizes $\frac{1}{r}-1$	(3) True rate of profit, $\frac{1}{r}-1$, for maximizing value of n
10%	7	15 4%
25%	5	34.9%
30%	4	41.1%
50%	4	64 8%

treated as capital expenditures at all), it may be inferred that the effect of the profit rate criterion, when profits are calculated in the manner described, is to discriminate in favor of long-term projects.

This apparent discrimination in favor of long-term investment, which would seem, among other things, to violate usual considerations of discounting future expectations for uncertainty, may be counterbalanced to some extent by the effects of calculations involving the pay-off or pay-out period, which involve a clear bias *against* long-lived properties. For assuming, as is reasonable, that depreciation charges are included in the returns estimated for pay-off of invested capital, shorter-lived assets have a better chance of meeting any given pay-off requirements than have longer-lived assets, in which annual depreciation charges are of course relatively less.

Flexibility and Time Lags

Interviews conducted for this study pointed to a variety of lags from stimulus to expenditure which may be relevant in economic analysis, particularly that part of analysis relating to cyclical fluctuations. Knowledge of these lags may also aid in determining the extent to which expenditures may differ from plans as economic conditions change. However, it would be presumptuous to offer general evaluations on the role of lags on the basis of the scattered bits of data collected in this study.

One lag to which the interviews called the writer's attention is that from the borrowing of money to its utilization in capital expenditures. This lag may apparently be fairly long. To the extent that it is, efforts to control the rate of investment by manipulating the money market and/or the rate of interest involve a serious complication, in addition to other difficulties suggested by economists in recent decades.

Among the scattered bits of data of some interest (but probably little surprise) is the information that the reaction of capital expenditures to a change in demand will depend upon how long the changed rate of demand is expected to continue. There was further evidence that the continued existence of a new rate of demand in the present was frequently a crucial basis for the expectation that the new rate of demand would continue in the future. What this signifies is that firms may not be quick to adjust capital expenditure plans to changes in demand.

In addition to the delay from the time of stimulus to the completion of a decision by management to make capital expenditures or to alter the rate of capital expenditures, a delay which is sometimes related to a shortage of entrepreneurial or management services, there may be further delays incident to acquiring funds, making arrangements with suppliers, and securing or putting to work appropriate personnel.

Finally, major capital expenditures frequently involve construction which takes place over a substantial period of time — perhaps several years. Firms appear generally reluctant to abandon projects in midstream. Thus there was evidence that the 1949 economic recession resulted more in delay of new expenditures than it did in cessation of expenditures on projects which had been initiated before the dip but were not yet completed.

Business respondents tended to think of curtailment of expenditures as a delay or suspension rather than as an abandonment. In the sense that the long-run trend for virtually all firms has been upward, they were undoubtedly correct. But neither this nor the evidence that projects already commenced would be dropped only with considerable reluctance may properly be interpreted as signifying that investment would hold up well in the face of a serious drop in the general level of economic activity. Indeed, a number of respondents boasted of their "flexibility" and ability to curtail sharply where necessary.

The lag in expenditures due to shortages and order backlogs of suppliers appeared such as to lead in some cases to a curiously perverse movement of capital expenditures in the face of a generally adverse turn in the economic climate. For in the event of a general drop, suppliers may have many cancellations, reducing their backlogs and enabling them to fill much more rapidly than anticipated the orders which have not been canceled. This results in a telescoping of expenditures into a briefer period by those firms which do not cancel. Thus firms which do not cancel orders may actually increase their own capital expenditures in the face of a general decline which they feel able to weather without major changes in plans.

Accuracy of Estimates and Reaction to Surveys

The interview findings offered some insight into factors in changes in investment plans and reasons for discrepancies between anticipated capital expenditures, as reported to surveying organizations, and the expenditures which actually occurred. A tendency of survey respondents to list only those expenditures definitely planned was found. This occasions a serious underestimate when the period under consideration is near the planning horizon of the firms responding. The underestimate is probably accentuated by the sharp distinction made by many firms between "planned" and "approved" expenditures; the horizon of the latter is of course very near and many firms insist that no formal plans (such as might be utilized by reporting controllers) contain other than approved expenditures. However, the interviews also indicated certain tendencies to overestimate expenditures. These may stem from the incentive to operating people to make high cost estimates in order to avoid having to justify requests for supplementary appropriations because original grants prove inadequate. Tendencies to overestimate expenditures may result also from the peculiar personal position of the respondent. For the person furnishing "the firm's" anticipations is frequently the controller, for whom capital expenditure estimates are merely part of cash forecasts or cash budgets in which he is under some pressure to be "conservative." To be conservative, in this context, means to underestimate receipts and to overestimate expenditures.

In addition, one must note that a substantial number of respondents apparently are led to make estimates which they do not expect to prove accurate. These relate, in particular, to the timing of capital expenditures. There is frequently little advance knowledge of exactly when projects will be completed, and when bills will fall due or be paid. Thus, quarterly and even annual estimates of future capital expenditures by individual firms may prove to be in substantial error not because any expenditures are actually canceled or because new ones are incurred but simply because expenditures are not incurred in the particular period predicted. In regard to the preparation of quarterly estimates, in at least one case the survey respondent reported that he simply arbitrarily calculated one-fourth of his annual estimates. In a number of cases, interviewees stated that they did not reply to questions asking them to estimate future expenditures because they did not know what the future rate of expenditure would be.

Conclusion

Finally, the writer must caution again that the positive ideas suggested in this analysis are tentative. They are offered for scrutiny, pondering, and possible verification, not merely by others employing interview techniques, but by the body of economists studying capital formation with whatever tools may be at their command. For perhaps the one definite conclusion that this writer may allow himself is the essentially negative one that the interview technique cannot by its nature, in an area of this kind, be definitive. It can suggest ideas and theories, offer new insights into relationships uncertainly grasped. But explanation and prediction of economic variables must finally receive confirmation in the operation of those variables themselves, and not in the subjective explanations of those who presume to control them.

With our various methodological strictures and this concluding reservation in mind, we may now turn to the detailed firm-by-firm reports which constitute the remainder of this paper.

IV. INDIVIDUAL FIRM REPORTS

Firm A (Farm Equipment)

This is a large multi-product firm primarily engaged in manufacturing agricultural equipment; the company underwent a very substantial expansion both in sales and in size of plant in the years following the end of World War II. Probably well over half of current plant and equipment (valued at original cost) has been acquired since the war.

Although interviews took place on a number of occasions in 1952 and once in 1954, most of the information relating to capital expenditures was secured from one official and from firm documents. The official, whose responsibilities were in the financial and accounting field rather than in production or merchandising, will be referred to generally as "the respondent."

The respondent reported that major postwar capital expenditures went into "facilities for several new products and for model changes to existing products as well as facilities to take advantage of technological changes in manufacturing — better materials and handling equipment, for example — and new distribution facilities, including depots for parts distribution."

Estimates of productive capacity requirements are derived from figures for "normal demand" developed by a special staff department. Normal demand is interpreted as the quantity of product the company can expect to make and sell in 7 out of 10 years.[24] After the war a special new plants committee was set up.[25] Major expansion decisions, it was reported, were based in the final analysis on the evaluation of the company president after full consideration of all pertinent factors as presented by this committee.

There was further evidence that substantial expenditures were not

---

[24] A 1947 memorandum declares:
"Following is the concept of the 'Company Normal Level Estimate' —
'The "Normal Level Estimate" is a carefully measured analysis of total annual product requirements, anticipated to meet composite requirements of all sales departments the majority of years out of a ten year period.
'The "Normal Level" reflects a mean quantity for each item during a ten year normal period It does not represent quantities for any specific year but indicates a level of sales which the Company can expect to achieve seven out of ten years under normal conditions The "Normal Level" is a measure for use in establishing production facilities. It provides a means for long range planning'"

[25] It consisted of the controller (later executive vice-president), the vice-president in charge of manufacturing and his assistant, the vice-president concerned with inventories, the treasurer, the industrial engineer, the construction manager, the assistant controller, and such other personnel as seemed appropriate for the particular projects under consideration.

undertaken hastily. Referring to a major expansion in production of a particular type of tractor, involving expenditures of several tens of millions of dollars, the respondent pointed out that three months before the expansion was decided upon, the attitude of top management could be described as "Well, we'll wait until new tractors come out. This may be a temporary flare-up in demand." Expansion was undertaken only when management was convinced that the upsurge in demand was not temporary.

Nature and Extent of Estimates and Plans

The capital expenditure program for several future years is listed in a document drawn up quarterly by the assistant controller and sent to top management. Items included arē at least approved in principle by management. In May, 1950, this document listed the capital expenditure program in detail, item by item, by year of estimated expenditure, from 1950 through 1954.

Expenditures listed for 1952 and 1953 in the May, 1950, document totaled almost 50 percent less than those listed for 1951; those listed for 1954 were, in turn, about 30 percent less than those listed for 1953. This tapering off occurred despite the inclusion of a constant item through these years for "non-programmed items to be appropriated — per budget," which by 1954 accounted for over half of the May, 1950, estimate. "We recognize," the respondent explained, "that amounts shown for the later years in the budget are light because we know additional things will come in that we don't now foresee."

A similar report, drawn up in July, 1951, listed the capital expenditure program from 1951 through 1954, thus projecting forward one year less than the earlier document. The July, 1951, estimates for 1952 and 1953 ran some 70 percent higher than the May, 1950, estimates for these years. The 1951 estimate for 1954 was about 40 percent higher than its 1950 counterpart. However, the July, 1951, estimate for 1951 was some 35 percent less than the forecast which had been made in May, 1950. Comparison of the first (May, 1950) and second (July, 1951) reports thus appears to confirm the respondent's statement that the capital expenditure program does not spring into being, full-blown, but grows over time as additional items appear desirable. (The mid-1951 estimate turned out to be 15 percent under the actual 1951 capital expenditure figure given in the company's annual report. On the other hand, actual 1951 capital expenditures were 30 percent less than had been estimated in May, 1950.)

Thus, over and above this tendency for the program to grow with the passage of time, one notes an instability of annual capital expenditure estimates as well as a failure of estimates to correlate highly with actual expenditures. Both of these characteristics reflect in part uncertainty as to the date when approved or programmed expenditures will actually be made. They may also be accounted for in the documents we have been considering by the particular period involved: the beginning of the Korean War. The company's anticipated sales for 1952, as broken down in the 1951 document, involved a very substantial increase under the heading "Defense Sales — Major Contracts."

The 1951 document prepared by the assistant controller also projected estimates of selected income statement and balance sheet items (including sales and inventories) for 1951 and 1952. An internal memorandum discussing the accuracy of financial estimates pointed out that these estimates "reflected uniformly a *conservative* viewpoint," and that cash positions in 1948, 1949, and 1950 turned out considerably better in each case than had been forecast in first quarter estimates. Capital expenditures, it was noted, had been overestimated for each of these years; the overestimates ran to about 40 percent, 20 percent, and 40 percent of the actual expenditures for 1948, 1949, and 1950, respectively.

In 1954, the respondent reported that the firm now carried estimates for the current year and three years ahead instead of for the current year and four years ahead (as in the May, 1950, report). This reduction in the length of forward estimates, he said, was made because the figures for the fourth year involved a period so far in the future that there was not much certainty about it.

Capital expenditure plans are taken very seriously, it was explained. When an item goes to the board of directors for approval, the board is informed whether the item is "on the program." If it is already in the program or plan it is likely to go through. The capital budget, which is revised and presented to the board every quarter, "is really a plan."

In most cases, capital expenditures in this firm run less than the amounts appropriated, apparently because the company does not permit "overrunning" an appropriation. In estimating capital expenditures against appropriations already made, however, the respondent declared the controller's office takes account of the tendency not to use up appropriations.[26]

In addition to "Statement 3-A," listing the capital expenditure program for the current and future years, the assistant controller submits "Statement 3-B," including "Projects Considered Desirable But Beyond Financial Limits of Present Program" and "Statement 3-C," enumerating "Projects Requiring Further Study (And Not Provided For In Present Financial Program)." Items in Statement 3-B, the respondent explained, were those accepted in principle but not to the extent that they were included in financial planning. In the case of Statement 3-C, there was less confidence that items listed would eventually be carried through. For example, it was pointed out, on one occasion a sale-lease program was listed which did not finally develop. Some of the items in the 3-B and 3-C lists will be moved up to the definite program (3-A) in later years. Some are considered for action only in case of possible market situations. If the appropriate situations do develop, they will get on the definite program.

Formal Aspects of Approval

The "Appropriations Regulations and Procedures" indicate that capital expenditures may be under blanket or specific appropriations, with certain other expenditures under minimum amounts allowed to local managers.

Blanket appropriations may be employed for all maintenance and replacement expenditures except "(a) when they are costly and occur only at rare and irregular intervals, or (b) when they are of the nature of rebuildings (which for tax purposes may require special accounting treatment) or (c) when there is a real question whether they might be classed as improvements." It is stipulated that

Blanket appropriations are intended to cover only normal expenditures for maintenance, replacements. etc. and not new installations. By new installations is meant both the requirements for new locations and special installations of equipment required for major changes in office methods. . . . All blanket appropriation requests for a given year are to be considered at the

---

[26] It was remarked, in 1954, that preparation was under way on an estimate of "underexpenditure to be turned back at 5 per cent" — presumably the difference between actual expenditures and 95 percent of authorized expenditures on specific items. The capital expenditure projections submitted by the assistant controller, it should be noted, include a subtraction labeled "Estimated underexpenditures to be turned back — 5%," which is equal to 5 percent of the total expenditures listed for each year.

same meeting of the Board of Directors, usually the October meeting in the prior year.[27]

All expenditures other than those included under blanket appropriations and certain minor expenditures which can be made at the discretion of local managers require specific individual appropriations. The board of directors retains authority for approval of all large appropriations (over a certain specified amount equal to about two-tenths of 1 percent of the company's annual expenditures). Authority for approval of smaller appropriations is delegated, with the "limit of authority" for approval graduated in accordance with the rank of the approving officer. Thus, appropriations which are large, but less than the amount requiring board approval, may be authorized by the president or, in his absence, by the designated vice-president. Lesser amounts may be approved by vice-presidents; still smaller amounts by any executive officer, the director of manufacturing, the director of engineering, or the general manager of a division; and so on down the line.

Procedure for getting approval of specific appropriations varies with the size of the appropriation. In the case of appropriations requiring approval at a vice-presidential level or higher, covering letters setting out the reasons for the request are required. Still larger appropriations, requiring approval of the president or the board, are subject to special checking by an "Appropriations Review Committee" which was recently set up and which works under the direction of the vice-president in charge of manufacturing. The "Appropriations Regulations and Procedures" state:

On major projects which have been favorably received in principle by the management, either after Product Committee action or special conference, the assistance of the Appropriations Review Committee should be requested before final figures are embodied in an appropriations request. The Committee will review the appropriation plan as to production methods contemplated, possible use of other Company facilities and other features. Preliminary approval by this Committee will be necessary before the project can receive the endorsement of the Vice President in charge of manufacturing — which in turn is required before the proposal is approved by the President or the Board of Directors.

---

[27] Blanket appropriations are used, it is reported, for:

"District office, parts depot and transfer repairs, maintenance and minor additions.

Service station equipment replacements and additions.

Office furniture and equipment replacements and minor additions for all locations.

Pallets for parts depots and transfers.

District office trucks.

Company signs for all locations, when such are to be purchased outright."

Among the reasons for requesting appropriations are the following:
1. Addition of a new production, distribution, or service facility.
2. Addition of a new product, or product line.
3. Increase in production schedules.
4. Necessity of equipment for bringing out a new model or making design changes.
5. Necessary replacement of worn out equipment.
6. Unusual or extraordinary maintenance.
7. Overhauling or rebuilding machine tools.
8. Cost reduction by replacing machinery or equipment with that of a more efficient kind.
9. Cost reduction by plant rearrangement programs and/or mechanization of production or processes.
10. Cost reduction by providing facilities to manufacture components presently purchased.
11. Improvement of working conditions.

Where expenditures are requested for more than one of the purposes listed above, the covering letter is to indicate how much of the request is related to each of the following purposes:

>Expansion of activities
>Replacements to maintain schedules
>Unusual maintenance
>Improved working conditions or safety
>New models or design changes
>Cost reduction or savings.

In the case of new models or design changes, appropriation requests are required to indicate approval by the "Product Committee." With regard to requests in whole or in part for the purpose of cost reduction or savings, there is to be an estimate of the "annual cost reduction or operating savings" expected.

The Role of Expansion

The question of the level of long-term demand has been of most significance in capital expenditures for expansion purposes. This is brought out, with some interesting implications for the role of uncertainty, in the problem of expansion in the production of a certain type of tractor. For, the respondent declared, although "our capacity has been inadequate in this tractor in post-war years," there has been "difference of opinion as to the level of long-term demand." The company has been slow to expand capacity in this product because:

1) The relevant plant is on a limited area where expansion is not physically feasible. To expand capacity it would be necessary to build a new plant on another site.

2) Other important projects were being carried out which were felt to have more urgency.
3) The . . . department [which estimates future demand] has not been firmly enough convinced that there was that additional long-term demand.

Related to action taken to meet the expected long-term demand is the question of a desirable percentage of capacity at which to operate. The respondent reports again:

The opinion of our President is that it is most desirable to be bulging at the seams. . . . I would say that in most of our plants good profits come at 80 to 90 per cent of capacity.

What then are the restraints on operating at a high percentage of capacity?

We calculate that we lose 10 or 15 per cent of normal day-shift production on the 2nd shift and up to 30 per cent on a 3rd shift because of lower efficiency. The third shift, we say, right off the bat, is unfeasible. Our postwar planning was based on our assembly lines running only one shift (which ties with shipping), and the machining departments working two shifts to feed the assembly lines. Then to run the assembly lines a second shift, machining operations have to be farmed out.[28]

If the company is faced with an increase in demand, then

Within certain limits we can add manpower. We would not add new equipment if within limitations of plant layout we could add hours or manpower. The question of what to do goes back to the difficulty of making estimates as to the future. . . . How far to go in the direction of expansion as against an increase in employment is based on the evaluation of long-run forecasts.

New Products

Capital expenditures are made in some magnitude in order "to keep up the product line." In regard to this type of expenditure, a significant factor is, in the words of the respondent,

. . . whether you're gaining or losing in the market. Where an old product (as . . . tractors) was holding up in sales, meeting demand satisfactorily, we desisted in introducing change. . . . We endeavor to anticipate changes in sales and demand; we try to have new product ready *before* a product declines or to be ready as soon as it declines.

It is unusual, however, to have such a delay in introducing a new model that machine tools specific to the model wear out before they become obsolete because of a change in model. The replacement of

---

[28] It was explained that some plants used to run one shift of machining with one shift of assembly work or two shifts of both. But the postwar period saw a swing to two-shift machining and one-shift assembly operations. This change was ascribed to the increase in premium wage rates for non-day shifts.

such specific machine tools is sometimes held back in anticipation of a new model in order to reduce obsolescence.

New Locations

Moving to a new location is a substantial factor in capital expenditures but is frequently closely interwoven with motivations of modernization and expansion. Personnel situations are admittedly important in locational questions. The respondent stated:

One of the things which sometimes stops us from a move is the presence of a skilled and loyal supply of employees... Our experience in setting up ... new plants after the war — dealing with new people, new unions, "bugs," etc. — is not very conducive to moving.

Tax considerations, it was suggested, might influence locational decisions, for "high taxes encourage moves as high costs can be charged in a high profit, high tax period while efficient plant is made ready for later use."

The Role of Replacement

In regard to replacement the respondent asserted:

Of course, replacement and maintaining capacity are not the same. Everybody recognizes that almost all replacement improves things a bit. . . . The bulk of replacement is determined by immediate technological need. In regard to machine tools a replacement usually must eliminate the old tool. Sometimes in contemplating capital expenditures for a new product, it is planned to move old equipment to make service parts for the old product. Sometimes the old equipment is stored for some possible future use. Sometimes it is scrapped or sold.

The respondent stressed the difficulty of distinguishing between replacement and expansion. He declared:

It isn't always possible to say definitely how much of capital expenditures is for new products or expansion and how much is replacement. . . . We made a study a few years ago in response to a question by the company president to determine what capital expenditure would be necessary to maintain capacity as compared to depreciation charges. We came up with a figure . . . just to maintain existing facilities, 15 per cent above depreciation charges. . . . That does contemplate some expenditures because of technological change.

As to timing of replacement expenditures:

We are almost totally bound by circumstances. For example, in coke ovens (which need replacement after 20 or 30 years) we want to get full life. We'll appropriate to rebuild an oven when steel men think it has to be done.

In regard to expenditures to keep facilities up to date:

The business cycle could have some effect on our psychology. Since we're a large company, opportunities for technological advance tend to average out. Taking advantage of technological opportunities may vary with

1) General psychology (business cycle)
2) Competition with other projects
   a) Managerial limitations in sifting projects
   b) Engineering limitations in carrying out all of the projects at once
   c) Financial limitations.

On the matter of book depreciation, the respondent declared that he would not like to give the impression that this was considered important. Of much greater importance for a plant than the state of its depreciation account is its efficiency, he stated. However, as will be noted later, depreciation is charged on both old and prospective new equipment in estimating savings relative to requested capital expenditures.

In regard to the question of the adequacy of depreciation charges to cover replacement costs, the respondent declared that replacement cost for his company would not be markedly greater than original cost. This was explained in part by the fact that so much of the company's capital account is recent, involving property acquired in the relatively high price postwar period.

Supply Price — Costs of Construction and/or Equipment

The respondent tended to minimize the effect of price changes on investment plans. He stated that there had been

. . . only one case of deferring the building of a new plant because of construction costs and this was only one of several elements involved. Don't know of any curtailment of plans because of price rises. However, this may have happened at divisional level, where project was delayed. Price rises from inception to execution of project — 18 months — have not been enough to be of influence.

In a later interview (1954) the respondent explained that "price escalation money is ear-marked specifically. Thus we have anticipated the possibility that construction costs might go up. But we have done that in advance and provided for it."

Working capital is more important than plant and equipment expenditures in financial considerations, the respondent declared. Price increases of, say, 5 percent could give a much greater jolt in terms of working capital requirements than in terms of capital expenditures.

Cost of Capital

"Practically," the respondent maintained, variation in cost of capital does not influence capital expenditure decisions. He explained that "cost of capital" has a direct relation to the price of common stock, among other elements. He related capital cost to a "composite" of the costs of money acquired through common stock (where the cost was calculated as the ratio of earnings to the market value of stock), preferred stock, borrowing, and liabilities (which last would be counted as "no cost"). The treasury department (of the company), the respondent declared, figured the composite capital cost at 8 percent after taxes, but this he said was obviously a shifting figure.

Calculations

The "Appropriations Regulations and Procedures" outline

. . . some considerations which should be kept in mind in making cost savings estimates to be used in submitting appropriations requests. Such estimates are regularly called for where appropriations are requested on a savings basis. This includes plant rearrangement programs or adoption of more efficient manufacturing methods involving possibly substitution of mechanical for hand processes. It also includes cases where a proposal is made to manufacture some component previously purchased. Perhaps the largest number of cases where cost savings estimates must be made involve equipment replacements. . . . Cases will occur where equipment replacements are essential to maintain production schedules. In many cases, however, the question of whether to replace or not, or the decision of *how* to replace, must be made on the basis of cost savings anticipated. It should be kept in mind that each appropriation request competes with other projects. The management of the Company, in choosing those which it will approve, does so with the objective of securing a maximum profit return from the funds which it has available for capital expenditure purposes. Accordingly, the management chooses those investment opportunities which offer the most attractive return.

Those making estimates are advised to base them on "realistic production schedules and not on some theoretical volume higher than that likely to be attained in the foreseeable future" since output "may be limited by demand." This last may indicate that demand for equipment for purposes of cost saving on replacement is not independent of those factors relating to business conditions and demand which influence capital expenditures generally.

Those making calculations of cost savings to be expected from replacement are instructed to include depreciation charges "on the old and the new machine" in comparing costs. However, in determining the amount of investment necessary for a replacement expenditure, salvage value of the old equipment is to be deducted from the capital requirement for the new equipment. In the case of old plant or equipment which would, upon replacement, have some other use within the company, salvage value of the old asset is to be counted as its depreciated book value. Otherwise, the depreciated value of the old equipment is to be ignored.

Illustrative examples of cost-saving calculations also make clear that in comparisons of present equipment and proposed replacements, depreciation charges are to be listed as costs on both. In fact, in one illustrative case, where no depreciation charge is listed for the present equipment, a footnote explains that "Present equipment is fully depreciated." This handling of depreciation charges as a cost over and above the original capital cost, and further, charging depreciation on both old and new equipment, it will be noted, is apparently a fairly widespread business practice, some of the implications of which were discussed earlier (pp. 29-34).

On "fairly simple projects where the proposed expenditure is relatively small," approval may usually be recommended "on the basis of the number of years it will require anticipated annual cost savings to equal the added investment." This "pay-off" basis should be used only, however, for "cases where the estimated annual savings, *before income taxes,* are sufficient to equal the added net investment in not more than 24 months. (This would mean, if we assume a long-time average of 50% effective income tax rate, those cases where, after income tax shrinkage of savings, the investment would not take more than 4 years to recover.)"

Where the anticipated pay-off period is longer, returns are to be estimated on a rate-of-profit basis, taking into account the "investment risk" due to

(1) possible decline of demand for products which the new equipment is intended to turn out — either absolute demand, or demand at a satisfactory price; and (2) possible technological improvements in production equipment which would render the new equipment obsolete. Management must decide the extent to which such risks are present and the extent to which they must be allowed for by increasing the percentage of return which is considered a fair objective.

The "Appropriations Regulations and Procedures" declare further:

It is recognized that a portion of the investment is recovered each year through depreciation provisions and logically the *average* investment over the depreciable period could be used as a base for the percentage of return. Because of the risks of rapid obsolescence, however, it is considered that the percentage of return during the early years is most significant and the

Company's policy is to use the more conservative approach of calculating percentage of return on the total added net investment, without adjusting for depreciation.

It may be demonstrated, however, that the objectives of conservatism and minimization of risk just expressed are not consistently effectuated by the calculating technique employed.[29]

Calculations of percentage return as a result of cost saving, we are told, are to be made without consideration of income taxes or risks. Matters of taxation and risk *are* to be considered by management in evaluating proposals. "Decision then should be made in the light of all these factors which indicate the over-all desirability of the project and permit it to be compared with other projects and the profit possibilities they afford."

Firm B (Farm Equipment)

This is another large firm in the farm equipment industry. A top vice-president writes (in answer to our terminal letter):

The basic planning of our company rests upon our ideas as to what product and how much of it we will be able to sell (a) within the near term (say, twelve months ahead) in terms of present facilities, and (b) for the long term (say, three to five years hence) in terms of the facilities we might need to achieve any goals in excess of existing capacity.

. . . . .

For the long term, it has to be recognized that we are part of the continuing process of mechanization. From the beginning of time, man has devoted a large part of his thinking toward ways and means whereby the load may be taken from his flesh and bone and placed upon inanimate but controllable material in the form of tools and machinery. This process is accentuated by such factors as population growth and increasing wage rates — because higher labor costs have the general effect of promoting the use and development of labor saving devices. In the light of such a background, therefore, we attempt to envisage as best we can the extent to which the total market might grow and the proportion of such market we might reasonably expect to attain. Plans are then devised to suggest what might be needed to achieve such an objective in terms of physical plant and permanent capital. If circumstances permit, these plans are then allowed to mature for awhile so that they may be considered continuously in the light of changing conditions and any developments having a bearing upon the subject.

At this stage, such a matter as personnel is given very little consideration for the reason that the creation of a work force would be an important element in the selection of a locality for expanded productive capacity.

---

[29] Note discussion on pp. 29-34 of the kind of bias introduced by giving expected life of capital only implicit recognition to the extent that it is involved in estimated depreciation charges.

Profitability would also be given limited consideration at this stage since experience has left us with a general indication that if we are able to participate effectively in a market within our field of endeavor, we are able to provide the customer with values in excess of our production costs, i.e., at a profit. Taxes also are of limited significance at such an early stage since we claim no ability to forecast the conduct of governments. We do, however, accept the premise that it is the job of business to succeed in spite of taxes. Nor would much consideration be given to the matter of prices since in long-term planning it has to be generally assumed that prices and costs, including wages, will tend to move in an approximately similar pattern.

The Role of Expansion

Discussions with the vice-president who wrote the foregoing, with the controller, assistant controller, and head of production scheduling tended to support and amplify this statement. This firm seems guided primarily by the belief that demand has been expanding through most of the firm's history and may be expected to continue to expand. Thus major capital expenditures have apparently constituted general expansion programs. The controller reported

control of expenditures by project once a general expansion program is set up. . . . After a general expansion program of a certain magnitude is approved the detailed projects to implement this plan are set up and controlled.

He declared further:

Expectation of continuation of current trend is the significant factor in immediate forward planning. Sustained high current demand leads to expectation of continuation of high demand. Most concerns do pretty well if they hit 80 per cent of capacity.

Capacity, the assistant controller volunteered, would be considered the output of three shifts working five days a week, although he explained, "Actually we operate less than full on second and third shifts and compensate by operating on Saturday." Relative employment on the three shifts is in the order of 5-3-2 or 5-3-1½, he reports. However, capacity in regard to assembly lines frequently involves one shift, and the entire firm's capacity for a single product may be determined by the output of one machine working seven days a week. The controller concluded, "Frankly, we don't know what total company capacity is precisely. It depends on the product mix."

In determining capital expenditures for expansion, the vice-president explained, capacity was not wanted for "peak demand."

We don't want over-full capacity for a short-term peak and a lot of idle capacity for the rest of the time. . . . Capacity is provided in terms of that amount which would permit us to satisfy a high level of demand without forcing us to develop too much backlog, or lose too much to competitors.

The controller confirmed suggestions by the interviewer as to the role of uncertainty, indicating that the relative certainty of anticipations was of great importance to expenditure decisions. On the structure of near-term sales anticipations, the head of production scheduling declared, "Generally speaking we produce what we expect to sell." The controller added, "Most people's predictions of tomorrow are just a continuation of today." When asked whether he meant the continuation of present level or the continuation of present rate of change, he replied: "When forecasting we tend to forecast continuation of the trend. The parts department certainly acts that way. When sales are going up it will demand even more." However, the head of production scheduling, thinking again perhaps of the uncertainty issue, stated: "We have so much capacity for . . . tractors. Any decision to increase that beyond piddling amounts would involve tremendous expenditures and would be a Board matter. . . . There is a general reluctance to expand permanently to meet a temporary shortage." The controller made the probably quite relevant statement, "It takes a very long time — now two years — to meet a shortage of capacity."[30]

Share of the Market

Share-of-the-market problems brought some interesting responses. Said the vice-president:

Quite apart from total industry demand, what will be the proportion between . . . [a few of the top firms in the industry, of which the respondent's firm was one]? One thing which we watch and don't publish is share of the market. That is very important and much underrated as a factor in business planning.

Right now we have a feeling that if demand slumps we will come out better than anybody else. We think customer preference is with us.

The controller asserted that the volume of capital expenditures is influenced by the action of competitors — each reacting upon the other.

The relation of the share-of-the-market factor to such an apparently

---

[30] A corroborative report on the role of expectations of future sales in determining capital expenditures is offered by the secretary of a third farm equipment company who volunteers, in a letter to the present writer, " . . The management of a farm machinery company is interested in the long term trend of sales and markets by territories and types of implements, for only by anticipating demands for several years ahead is it possible to determine whether to build a new factory or branch In addition, we must be aware of technological and cost factors, in order to determine into just what channels our production and sales program should be stressed "

unconnected economic theory as the acceleration principle may be found in the controller's statement that "If our share of the market were falling in a capacity market we would expand. If our share were falling in a falling or stationary market we might cut prices." The former situation is one in which production is proceeding at a capacity rate and the fall in market share is occasioned by the firm's inability to meet demand, coupled with a greater ability by other firms in the industry to meet this demand (or at least their own traditional share of the demand, with some of the demand for the industry's products then being lost to the entire industry). As suggested in Chapter III (p. 23), the share-of-the-market factor can thus be interpreted as meaning that a firm will expand to meet an increase in demand if the alternative were a permanent sacrifice in sales rather than a mere deferral to a future slack period. The rule-of-thumb for determining a permanent sacrifice in sales in a "capacity market" is a falling share in that market.

New Products

In regard to the distinction between investment in new products and in expanded facilities for the production of the old, the vice-president of this firm declared: "In the past year we have favored, where we had the choice, more of the same products rather than new ones. We would act differently if our present products were not as eminently satisfactory as they are." He added that the nature of the product did not generally call for complete or conspicuous model changes such as in the automobile industry, and that changes in model have not on the whole been great in capital requirements. Rather, heavy capital expenditures have been entailed in institution of really new products, as the construction of a plant to make available a different type of engine for some of the firm's products.

The Role of Replacement

In the period of the interviewer's initial contact with the firm, there was an unusual demand for all available productive capacity. This resulted in drastic limitations upon the retirement of old equipment. At this time the controller declared, "We are replacing when things fall apart. If replacement is planned, when replacement comes along the 'replaced' asset and its replacement are both used." The vice-president explained in correspondence some two years later, stressing that circumstances had changed since the earlier interview:

In 1952 we were in the midst of a combination of circumstances entailing

(1) pent-up demand in excess of productive capacity, and (2) long delays in procurement of new capital tools and equipment. At the same time, government preference for our products was forcing good commercial customers into our competitors. More output was, accordingly, most essential — and for the time being was more important than the lower unit costs which could be attained if obsolescent equipment could be replaced by modern machinery. It was not that we did not wish to make replacements. We couldn't. Whatever new capital equipment we could get was applied to *more* output on top of what we could get from continued use of old equipment.

But that has all changed now. New machinery and equipment is much more readily available and product demand is below capacity. Our replacement policies are, therefore, again in full force and effect — and to a greater degree than ever before.

Capital Supply Considerations

The vice-president declared in correspondence with the interviewer:

... As a general rule, we operating people submit projects designed to provide either more product or lower unit costs without particular regard to capital supply considerations. It is then the responsibility of the Board of Directors to prescribe how fixed capital shall or shall not be used.

... I might add that under any different method of operating it is difficult to see how a Board of Directors could be kept abreast of capital requirements and the reasons therefor. If anything, I would be inclined to believe that responsibility for *not* approving management-recommended investment could often be greater than responsibility for approval. After all, if management is good, it will not likely submit for board approval capital projects which are not sound investment opportunities. And if they are sound investment opportunities, it is not likely that a progressive board would wish to forego them.

Firm C (Steel)

Nature and Extent of Estimates and Plans

In relation to capital expenditures, the executive vice-president of this large integrated steel company asserted that although "We don't have long-run forecasts, we do have long-run construction plans. — How far ahead? Further than we live!" Such plans might entail possible uses of land under company control. The executive vice-president declared, "These plans run thirty or fifty years ahead. They are not fixed, of course. But when we fill in a little part we can have a picture of the whole." He added, "I don't have too much faith in long-run forecasts. Things depend on national and international developments."

However, concerning the nearer future, the executive vice-president of the large steel firm stated: "We have . . . dollars of expenditures in mind [not in a plan] that could be done in the next five years if we elect to do them. We seldom appropriate more than . . . dollars [about one-fourth of the first amount]." On the very near future he remarked, "You can always anticipate expenditures a year ahead. . . . The year after is not so easy."

Formal Aspects of Approval

The executive vice-president offered two examples of the process of capital expenditure decision-making in approximately the following terms:

The firm is currently undertaking two major capital expenditure projects: basic steel capacity expansion and cost reduction in tin plate and cold rolled sheets. In the first case, in order to feed the finishing operations and maintain our place in the industry a 20 per cent expansion was decided upon. Engineering and operating people were then asked how to accomplish this. After consultation with company executives the proposal was taken to the board of directors and approved. In the second case, the project stemmed from the operating and engineering people. They're always concerned with matters of this kind. They evolved proposals which were taken to the vice president in charge of production. He took them to the president, who gave them back to the executive vice president to be checked and studied. The executive vice president then recommended the project to the president. He will in turn recommend it to the executive committee, supported in this by the executive vice president. It will go finally to the board of directors.

The executive vice-president declared that this firm had no budget for capital expenditures but did have one for maintenance and repair expenditures. This may reflect the fact that budgets are of prime use as guides in day-to-day decisions made by lesser officials while capital expenditures proper tend to be of major magnitude and importance, requiring top management action. This hypothesis may find confirmation in the report of the assistant treasurer of this large steel firm that all capital expenditures are approved either by the full board of directors or by its executive committee. The full board meets quarterly; the executive committee meets every month that the board does not meet but its decisions are subject to board review and ratification. Major programs are always held for board consideration.

The Role of Expansion

The decisive factor in major expansion expenditures is the firm's estimate of its future demand. This seems to run partly in terms of expected demand in the industry and partly in terms of how this firm's demand will vary as a share of the industry demand. The industry demand, as indicated, is viewed as determined by broad national and international political developments which management finds it difficult to predict. However, a definite view is expressed that national steel capacity should be adequate for some time to come, barring a general war, and that this company does not (spring, 1952) expect that eventuality. In terms of the company's share of the industry's market, management compares the growth in general output of the area and section served by this company and the growth in other areas served primarily by other companies. In addition, there is some attempt to evaluate the business and needs of present and prospective customers of the firm. This relates to new customers entering the area, to old ones expanding, and to anticipated actions of competitors in the area or section in which the firm concentrates its sales.

Explaining his own expectation of the future, the executive vice-president said he anticipated a "competitive market." He added,

By 1954 we will have an ingot capacity of 124 million tons nationally. If the country goes at 80% of capacity as in an ordinary good period, we think we could sell 100 per cent in this area. If nationally we ran at 60 or 70 million tons for five or six years and locally at 70 or 80 per cent we'd change our expectations and cut our expenditures.

Asked why he picked the "five or six years" figure, he came back to the long-run view so frequently found relevant to capital expenditures, "You'd have to have a belief that demand was keeping up to undertake a major expansion. Our present program was approved in the summer of 1950 and if business had gone to pot, we would have gone ahead. We would have thought the recession temporary." Again, confirming this with a statement about the past, "We came to realize about 1949 that we were on a new plateau and that we had to expand steel capacity. It took four years to accept this expectation."

An acceleration of need for capital expenditures as capacity is approached results from the increased demand for scrap and consequent necessity to develop new iron capacity to replace the unavailable scrap. The executive vice-president explained:

We're putting in this new steel capacity now and not expanding our iron capacity. If we did the latter we would have to expand blast furnaces, coke ovens, ore boats, mines, etc. . . . *I* believe we don't need it at this juncture. I believe the country will not require all this steel and hence scrap will be available. . . . Nobody really has trouble getting scrap when the industry is at 80 per cent or 90 per cent [of capacity]. Even at 100 per cent *we* have been able to get scrap without real trouble. If we had the experience for at least a year that we couldn't get scrap, I might change my mind on that.

Expansion and Cost Reduction

Several comments were offered by the executive vice-president to the effect that "Much expenditure is not for expansion, but rather for cost reduction and quality improvement. We expect a competitive market in regard to cost and quality of product." However, when the interviewer at this point suggested that these matters constituted the major factor in capital expenditures the response was "Also changes in industry demand."

Now the factor of unavailability of scrap may, of course, be revealed in high prices for scrap — prices so high as to necessitate construction of additional iron facilities. We may observe that this point is implicit in the executive vice-president's remark, pursuant to the statement just quoted, "We might also come to believe [that iron facilities would have to be constructed] in terms of cost reduction. I don't believe it will happen. In competitive times, scrap is cheaper."

It is instructive to dwell a moment on the last response. It might be quite likely that an analyst of questionnaire replies would tabulate this as pointing to cost reduction *rather than* pressure of demand as the factor bringing about capital expenditures. Yet it is clear upon careful examination that it is an increase in industry demand which might raise costs (of scrap) to a point that would force construction of facilities for an alternative source of pig iron. This may well be kept in mind in connection with a discussion of the entire concept of cost reduction versus expansion expenditures to which investigators in the area of capital expenditures have given considerable attention.

Calculations

The executive vice-president of this large steel company, discussing decisions on cost-reducing expenditures, declared: "There is no set formula that I know of. You ought to be able to make savings which return expenditure in ten years." But he gave no precise answer on how to calculate. He did volunteer that memoranda prepared for making such expenditure decisions would show the original cost of the project and the cost saving before taxes. "Who knows what will happen with taxes, or what to do with them in calculations?" he added. "I take a 50 per cent assumption on taxes. Thus, a four or five to one ratio looks good to me; I take it to be ten years after taxes." But "irrespective of ratios it's highly desirable for us to get on a competitive basis. We must be able to produce at as low a cost as competitors."[31]

---

[31] In later correspondence the interviewer asked: "What is the relative significance of this as a factor in capital expenditures as between periods when you are operating at capacity and periods when you are operating at below

The treasurer's office of this firm was of course somewhat more specific in discussion of the calculations of pay-off periods, earnings ratios, and the like but was still far from entirely definite. The assistant treasurer made available to the interviewer a two-page memorandum on the subject written by him for use in the plants. (This memorandum is reproduced on pp. 60-62). He indicated that accountants at plants did the calculations, including taxes in the computations. The assistant treasurer objected to inclusion of taxes because of uncertainty as to the excess profits tax. Items included in the calculations, he declared, were cost of the new equipment, salvage value of the old equipment if it were to be replaced, and cost of operating the present equipment (including depreciation charge, if any) compared with cost of operating the new equipment. The actual calculations generally involved a balancing of specific earnings and additional costs. The interest factor might or might not be considered; the assistant treasurer was not sure. Savings were estimated on an annual basis and divided into cost, perhaps on several different assumptions as to the percentage of capacity at which operations would be conducted. He thought that depreciation charges on the new equipment were generally included in the calculations but was not sure. When asked by the interviewer to comment on the inability of top management to explain pay-off calculations supposedly used in their companies, he indicated that top personnel did not get into the details of calculations; as long as they had a consistent measure they did not check further.[32]

---

capacity? And to what extent are decisions on cost-saving capital expenditures made on their own merits, regardless of the situations, actions or prospective actions of competitors?" The company president (formerly executive vice-president) replied:

"In my opinion, the necessity to bring costs down to 'a competitive basis' or lower if possible, is a strong influence on capital expenditures irrespective of whether the company is operating at capacity or below capacity. It may well be that greater attention is given to this problem in the latter periods when there is little necessity to expand, but prudence should dictate a continuing active interest in the subject. As far as our company is concerned, we are interested in spending capital to effect cost savings regardless of the situations, actions or prospective actions of competitors. Naturally, if a competitor develops a process which greatly lowers costs as compared with our own, it is a spur to action along similar or improved lines."

[32] In partial response to further inquiry as to methods of calculation, the company president wrote:

"It seems to me that you may be making too great an effort to blueprint the processes of determining capital expenditures. If they could always be done according to a specific formula, there would be very little need for individual judgment. However, in my opinion, once the facts are assembled, judgment as to the long-run value of the contemplated expenditure, all angles considered, is the determining factor."

Capital Supply Considerations

Cost and/or availability of capital appeared to be of some significance in determining the level of capital expenditures in this company. The executive vice-president volunteered that "we have no future plans. It will depend upon the situation and the availability of capital." In regard to the latter he added,

We would not want to change our financial position from strong to weak. We just borrowed 50 million dollars. We did that with plenty of thought and we'd want to consolidate our position before borrowing any more. You need a lot of money in this business without expansion at all. We spent 152 million dollars in six years, 36 million last year — much of it for modernization and rehabilitation, not expansion.

In view of the persistence of reports by investigators that cost of capital does not enter into investment decisions it may be useful to examine the manner in which this firm's executive vice-president views financial matters. Such an examination may suggest that at least some of the investigators getting negative responses on this issue are not raising questions in terms relevant to the businessman. This executive vice-president reported:

We made quite a study of indebtedness in relation to the capital structure. We don't think, broadly speaking, that debt should be more than one-third of the capital structure, or it might impair our emergency borrowing power and harm our position in the market where our securities are well-thought of.

At present you can't put out common stock and expect to have it pay its way. No company can put out stock today without diluting its old stock.[33] Our 50 million dollar loan should take care of capital needs for five years. We decided on the best way to get this: one-half in mortgage bonds and one-half in debenture bonds which could be converted to common stock. We may be diluting, but only mildly. . . . Later, in five or ten years, we can appraise the situation in the light of that time.

Different people have different ideas. Our company is conservative. Other companies, smaller than we, are borrowing much more.

The one to two ratio of debt to equity is not absolute [in answer to the interviewer's specific question on this matter]. If there were a terrific demand for steel in the industry and we felt we were losing our position in the industry, we might borrow more in order to enable us to maintain our position.

Lately capital expenditures have just about been fully covered by retained earnings and depreciation. However, of the 50 million dollar loan just

---

[33] The writer interprets "diluting its old stock" to mean reducing the value of existing stock by selling new stock, the returns from which will not, in the opinion of the market, be utilized to increase company earnings sufficiently to maintain the existing ratio of earnings to equity capital.

negotiated we anticipate using two-fifths for working capital and three-fifths for construction.

Careful examination of this statement should make it clear that although there is no direct evidence that interest rate cost, or even cost of capital in general, is significant, such considerations must be implicit in the concern about diluting stock and impairing the company's position in the securities market. For a high interest rate might well, *ceteris paribus,* necessitate higher yields to attract capital to new investment in equities. And resultant higher yields on old issues, granted the distaste for "diluting," tend to make additional capital look generally unavailable.[34]

However, to keep the role of capital supply in proper perspective, we may weigh the remarks of the assistant treasurer, who declared:

The question of availability of funds usually comes in at the tail end of the decision. After top management has about decided to go ahead, the issue of funds may come up. If funds are short, top management may be asked to take another look, or get new sources of funds.

Flexibility and Time Lags

On the question of time lags from decisions to actual expenditures and on the flexibility of plans as economic conditions change, matters of considerable importance in economic theory, it was not possible to get an answer susceptible of easy summary. One cost reduction project was reported by the executive vice-president to have "knocked around for nine months, another for a year or two. It all depends on how clean cut it is. If there are differences of opinion it may take long to get approval, and it may be rejected." If demand softens, whether proposed expenditures will be carried through depends on the nature of the expenditure — and, of course, on how long the drop in demand is expected to continue.

---

[34] One may still argue, it should be noted, that interest rate is relatively unimportant compared with expected profitability and the rest of the complex of factors influencing capital values. See J. M. Keynes, *General Theory of Employment, Interest and Money* (New York: Harcourt, Brace and Company, 1936) especially pp. 147-64.

EXHIBIT: MEMORANDUM FROM TREASURER'S OFFICE OF A LARGE STEEL FIRM
Re: *Request for Policy on Minimum Return on Investment Required for Justification of Proposed Expenditures*

Estimated return on investment does not, and cannot, properly evaluate all the factors involved in reaching a decision to approve or disapprove a proposed project, and consequently should not be used as the sole criterion on which to base such a decision.

Only a few of the other equally important considerations are mentioned here: (1) The relation of the project under consideration to long-range plans and policies of the company. A project estimated to provide a high return might involve expansion of capacity or change in output not deemed desirable in the long run, such as the installation of a pipe mill at the present time of shortage. (2) Factors not related to anticipated savings might justify a given project. For example, certain equipment might be installed to eliminate hazards to employees, even though no monetary savings resulted. Or smoke elimination equipment might be installed to protect community relations. (3) Maintenance of competitive position might dictate certain expenditures not estimated to yield a particularly attractive return. (4) Maintenance of production might require immediate replacement or additions to equipment which are not expected to result in decreased costs. (5) Funds may not be available no matter how great a return can be expected from the projects proposed.

It soon becomes evident that all pertinent factors must be considered in reaching a decision with respect to a given project.

It is believed that the last factor mentioned above, namely availability of funds, deserves special consideration. Obviously expenditures on plant and equipment are only one of several necessary applications of available funds which include maintenance of working capital position, dividends to stockholders and repayment of debt. The allocation of funds available internally from earnings and depreciation recovery, as well as the decision to procure funds externally by borrowing or as equity capital, are necessarily top management decisions. Because funds are not normally available in unlimited amounts for expenditure on plant and equipment, it is considered important that, insofar as possible, the expenditure of available funds be planned in advance in order to meet first those needs which are determined on the basis of all factors involved to be most immediate.

In advance planning of needs, distinction can properly be made between repair and maintenance expenditures and expenditures for improvements and additions to plant and equipment, since usually different emphasis is given in each case to the factors, other than estimated rate of return, involved. In the case of repair and maintenance expenditures, necessity is more likely to be the governing factor.

Through appropriate advance planning, proper control of such expenditures within the limit of available funds can more readily be achieved. Physical surveys of needs will enable classification of needs by priority on the basis of urgency and assist in the making of intelligent decisions on the basis of all factors including estimated rate of return.

Within the foregoing limitations, the estimated rate of return on a proposed investment can be useful as a guide in determining which expenditures should be made.

A basic rule to be borne in mind is that it should always be established that a proposed expenditure will result in savings over its productive life at least equal to the amount of the expenditure, thus permitting recovery from depreciation.

But because of the variety of factors other than rate of return involved, it is impossible to formulate a rule governing desired rate of return in excess of the break-even point that can be applied uniformly in all cases, and particularly in the case of major additions to plant involving the expenditure of large sums of money. In the case of projects of the size normally under consideration by the plant management, a suggested working rule would be to approve those projects in which the estimated savings will equal the cost of the project in three years or less, and to examine more carefully any projects failing to meet this rule. The three-year period is selected very arbitrarily on the grounds that it is the longest period during which the current cost factors forming the basis of the savings estimates are likely to continue unchanged. Application of the proposed rule should not mean automatic disapproval of projects failing to comply but rather provide opportunity for careful re-appraisal.

Since the future rate of return on a proposed investment can only be estimated, it is important that due consideration be given to the cost factors on which the estimate is based. In the first place, it is doubted that the decisions should be based on savings after income taxes, since this is an external factor not subject to plant management control, although it does bear directly on the amount of funds available for plant expenditures.

Secondly, it is desirable that the cost estimates used be prepared on a consistent and realistic basis since there is usually a tendency to overestimate on the part of the individual proposing the project. To assure the making of sound and consistent estimates, two specific controls are recommended. The first is establishment of a procedure whereby all estimates of rate of return are reviewed by an independent but qualified member of the accounting staff to assure that all pertinent cost factors are consistently taken into account. The second is establishment of a review procedure whereby the actual results attained following completion of a project are carefully compared with the estimates used for obtaining approval.

Firm D (Steel)

Nature and Extent of Estimates and Plans

This small steel company did not indicate as much in the way of long-run planning of capital expenditure possibilities as did the large company. The secretary-treasurer of the firm explained that in making estimates of future expenditures in connection with Commerce-SEC surveys and other questionnaires, he consulted with the president, the chairman of the board, and other responsible executives but added, "We're not very formal in this place... You take G. E. or Standard Oil of New Jersey and they have staffs to try to dope these things out. We don't have a staff to do that." The director of production planning (who had a well-developed procedure for the short-run process of production scheduling) declared, "I've found I'm not a good long-range planner. I cannot figure with certainty on the basis of what happened and my judgment of what will happen. I've found it undesirable to guess or plan ahead any further than I have to."

Formal Aspects of Approval

In regard to the method of deciding upon and approving capital expenditures, the president said:

We find out what the cost is. We say to the officers, this is it. Guess we need it. And that's about all. The Board of Directors finally approves capital expenditures of any sizable amount. Sometimes we accumulate quite a bit before the Board approves. Officers of the company are directors; there are only two outside directors. Expenditures are thus approved informally before they get to the Board.

Plant managers know our policies. [Hence they know what to do in regard to smaller expenditures.] Expenditures over five or ten thousand dollars would need approval. Before going ahead the plant managers would check with the vice-president in charge of manufacturing. Some large repair and remodeling expenditures would be approved by the Board. The vice-president in charge of production comes in with a list, perhaps totalling $180,000, which he has discussed previously.

The Role of Expansion

On the usually important need for expansion as a determinant of capital expenditures, the president of the small steel company had this to say:

Expansion of facilities — a rather simple thing! If equipment is worked seven days a week we figure something has to be done about it. We guess whether business will probably continue. We consider it may be a temporary boom but in the natural course of events the expansion will be warranted.

Criteria and Calculations

In determining whether to make capital expenditures, the president explained:

Somebody would have to calculate profit margins. Yes, he would look at profits on similar facilities. The decision on whether to make a large investment would depend on the profit margin. If you could get back your investment in a few years there would be less risk than if it would take ten or fifteen years.

Let's take one new item. Somebody came along with a patent. He had a lot of surveys. We checked with prospective users and others and it looked like a good market. We perfected a method of making the item, put in close to $300,000 over a period of two years. In the meantime, another method of performing the same operation came into the market and we found that instead of competing against an obsolete system, we were now competing with a product equal to or better than the product developed by us.

The company treasurer declared:

When we figure on installing an item of equipment we look at the potential profit. For example, on an item requiring substantial expenditures . . . we saw we could get back our investment in two to four years. It's the same way even in office equipment. There is no very set formula. Sometimes it is a question of replacing unavailable manpower, as with I.B.M. machines, which reduced the number of comptometer operators. . .

The treasurer claimed to have appropriate profits data available for all groups of commodities, with expenses allocated to each item of cost, but could not think of a project where prospective profit rates were actually calculated. He seemed inclined to explain this by the fact that general availability of profits data made it unnecessary to go through special calculations in regard to particular expenditures. In some cases expenditures would be made because "we have to have the capacity and we get it." More generally, "it would all depend on whether demand [for the product in question] would keep up." In regard to a major new foreign plant, considerations listed as significant were, "Save duty, labor probably less, and no union trouble."

Flexibility and Time Lags

On the question of lags and flexibility of decisions, the president declared, "We've made capital expenditures which began to produce just when business fell off." However, he added:

> We've stopped on some things. — We started on two plating machines. Then, when conditions didn't seem to warrant both any more, we only finished one and kept the parts on the other. We just finished it now. That was a $1.3 million project of which we stored $800,000 (generators, etc.) and left $500,000 to spend later.

The sense in which "conditions didn't seem to warrant both any more" is made clear by the explanation by the secretary-treasurer of the sequence of events and thinking in curtailment of capital expenditures:

> There was a definite drop in profits and volume amounting in 1949 to a drop of about 25 per cent in the tonnage of this item. That caused a lot of apprehension. We didn't need a second machine because it had been predicated on an expansion in demand.

Estimates and Surveys

One last point of interest to surveyors of planned capital expenditures may be mentioned. In discussion of his firm's reports in the Commerce-SEC surveys, the secretary-treasurer asserted that there is "no real way of anticipating quarterly expenditures." How did he get quarterly figures to report? He generally divided the annual estimates by four.

Firm E (Beer)

Extent of Capital Expenditure Plans

The controller of this national brewery, shipping beer throughout the nation, reported the existence of a three-year capital expenditure program as late as 1949-51. However, since 1952 the program has been projected for only one year. Excluding expansion by new breweries, the company has reached the point where capital expenditures for normal replacements and minor expansion projects will about equal annual depreciation charges. One may infer from this that long-run estimates of capital expenditures were abandoned when these expenditures became a relatively minor item in the company's financial picture.

Formal Aspects of Approval

The controller explained that all projects are screened by a plant committee. If the plant committee approves the project, it is then presented to the appropriations committee, which has authority to appropriate funds within limits set by the board of directors, and to authorize work to be started. If projects exceed the limits, authority to proceed with work is granted and appropriation of funds is made by the board of directors or its executive committee.

The board of directors approves the capital expenditures program early in the calendar year but "actual authorization of funds will be made only when projects come up for review."

Expansion and Cost Reduction

The bulk of recent heavy capital expenditures has been for "expansion and modernization," including construction of a new plant. However, the controller suggested that additions to the capital expenditure program are favorably considered when expenditures "will result in cash savings in one and one-half years or two years from three sources: 1) getting greater productivity with the same manpower; 2) reducing manpower; 3) using different materials (say, packages, cartons or fillers) which would reduce costs."

The Role of Replacement

Discussing the concentration on replacement expenditures, the controller confirmed the oft-noted interconnection between replacement and expansion with the statement, "In such cases the older piece of equipment is replaced with a larger piece which will carry a heavier load."

Calculations

The controller reported that the subject of criteria and calculations relating to capital expenditure decisions may be described generally as follows:

There is no set figure for the anticipated rate of return on contemplated capital expenditures as different items pay off at different rates. When a capital expenditure is submitted for approval, the request includes an analysis of increase in operating expenses or estimated savings. . . . Some projects will return the capital investment in one year, some three years, some five years, and some ten years. There are also capital expenditures which are never returned in the sense of increased efficiency, savings, or profits, but must be made for safety reasons, compliance with building codes, etc. I believe that it is a generally accepted rule that a capital investment which pays out in 5 to 7 years is considered excellent, and one which pays out in 7 to 10 years is considered good.

Capital Supply Considerations

The controller reported that there are occasions when the urgency of a project does not permit completion of all detail drawings before the project is started. In those cases the engineering department submits the best possible estimate of the cost of the project when asking for authority to proceed.

The controller explained that there were three methods of financing: (1) retained earnings; (2) long-term debt; and (3) equity financing (stock issues). The cost of financing, and its relation to income taxes, is considered when funds are derived from borrowing or sale of stock.[35] Every company tries to keep the cost of financing capital expenditures as low as possible, the controller asserted, but there are times when an expansion program must proceed even though the financing costs are higher than expected.

Firm F (Beer)

This firm is a fairly large, well-known regional brewery. Interviews were made with the company's treasurer (and assistant secretary), chief accountant, and chief of production scheduling. The treasurer explained that the "capital expenditure program is just about completed," revealing that two major expansions in cities other than that of the home office were either finished or near completion. "We don't plan on more expansion in the near future," he added. "For one thing, costs are too high."

Nature and Extent of Capital Expenditure Plans

The chief accountant referred to a five- to eight-year plan to expand three major plants, beginning about 1945, but at another point in the discussion asserted: "In the strict sense, I don't think that we have capital expenditure 'plans.' We've generally had a project, borrowed money for it, then had another project." At still another point in the discussion he stated that "as far as capital expenditures are concerned, the big major items are governed by a set program which we already know about."

---

[35] The report prepared by the controller's staff, "Summary of Capital Expenditure Projects in Progress as of March 31, 1952," has as column headings: (1) amount authorized; (2) cash required to complete; (3) cash expended in 1952; (4) cash requirements for balance of 1952; (5) estimated cash requirements in 1953 The data included are broken down by the product and service divisions of the company When a new plant is under construction, it appears as a separate item until completion.

Formal Aspects of Approval

The routine of approval on capital expenditures involves a "job system" on all items over $1,000, which are submitted by department heads for approval. Thus, according to the chief accountant, they "go through the people who do the work. They finally reach the general manager who can approve anything up to a major expansion, which may involve consulting with the President or Board of Directors."

Expansion

Some notion of the perspective involved in expansion decisions may be grasped from the following statement of the chief accountant:

These forecasts aren't made in the story-book fashion you might expect. A lot of them transpire over a year or two; they're forgotten about and then some time later somebody gets interested again.

The 1944-45 decision to expand was one of those favorable deals where you didn't have to think very hard. It didn't take bright minds to know we'd be able to sell all we could produce. Distributors were taking all we could sell.

Expansion and Cost Saving

Turning to the question of determinants of capital expenditures, we get some interesting material on the relationship between cost reduction and expansion expenditures. The chief accountant explained that the postwar "expansion was intended 1) to take care of increased demand of distributors and 2) to maintain established dock price without costly freight differentials to make up shortages." Again, explaining that a small brewery had been purchased some years before "to get some quick production," the firm had "always had in mind getting rid of it as quickly as possible because of the freight differential and because it was not efficient. Thus there were two expansions: 1) to take care of demand and 2) to make operations more efficient." Finally, the chief accountant declared specifically, "the expansion beginning about 1949 and just almost completed was primarily to reduce costs."

Expansion and Capital Supply Considerations

Periodic reports are prepared on the source and disposition of funds. Forecasts are made of the company's cash position, going ahead six months to two or three years, "according to needs," with an expansion program one of the factors that would necessitate longer-run forecasts. Such forecasts are apparently tied to the problem of convincing

banks of the desirability of extending loans. Thus, in soliciting a loan for expansion purposes, according to the chief accountant, the firm prepared various statements: such as pro forma balance sheets and anticipated earnings from new plant, for the purpose of meeting the questions:
1. Is the expansion going to pay? What will earnings be?
2. What will cash position be? Will there be enough cash?
3. In borrowing the money will we be able to pay off the loan?
We have to be able to show something to the bankers. At time of the last loan we took data to the bankers to show the expansion would be worthwhile, to prove it would result in increased earnings, and to prove our ability to pay off the loan.

The chief accountant explained further, "On a projected loan of two million dollars annual savings of well over one million dollars were estimated." However, the interviewer did not learn just how these "savings" were calculated. A view of the scope of interest rate considerations may be had from the following:

In making the loan we were trying to sell the banks on it. This was the time Korea had started up and banks weren't too enthusiastic about making loans. It wasn't so much a question of interest rates or terms of payment as convincing banks. This loan was primarily for more efficient operations to increase earnings.

Investigators have frequently interpreted remarks of this type to indicate that availability of bank loans is a basic determinant of capital expenditures. However, the context of the preceding statement may suggest that failure of a bank to grant a loan may stem from poor earnings and/or poor sales prospects of the company. The bank action would thus be the result of other determinants of investment rather than a basic determinant itself.

Accuracy of Estimates and Reaction to Surveys

The firm indicated substantial discrepancies between estimates and actual expenditures. These appeared to involve increases in costs, changes in the physical nature of projects, and failure to complete projects on schedule. Successive estimates on several major expansions showed a substantial rate of increase. Thus one plant expansion showed a $626,000 estimate in 1944, an $846,000 estimate in 1946, and a $912,000 estimate in May, 1947. Another plant expansion showed similar estimates of $2,460,000, $2,942,000, and $3,187,000 respectively. These projects were to be completed in January, 1948. They were actually completed about June 30, 1948. There appeared generally to be a period of roughly two years from the beginning of projects to their completion. Some discrepancy in regard to dates of expenditures developed in discussions between the interviewer and several officials of the company. The chief accountant ascribed this to differences between dates of inception or construction and dates of payment.

There was evidence of some confusion in regard to the firm's role in capital expenditure surveys. Discussing the Commerce-SEC reports, the chief accountant stated that for expenditures "on anything in the way of major expansion we'd know pretty well in advance. On replacements we might have to guess and be pretty far out on timing." But a bit later in the interview he revealed that no anticipated figures were furnished to the Securities and Exchange Commission. He also declared, "It seems to me that we do respond on McGraw-Hill." But a check by his assistant later revealed no reports to McGraw-Hill in the company files.

Firm G (Containers)

This firm is a very large one in the paper and cardboard container field. A basic consideration in regard to capital expenditures in the industry is revealed in the statement of the firm's president that "We have a twenty-five year or over per capita growth of six per cent in the paperboard field." One may infer that long-term views rather than short-term expectations are relevant to capital expenditures from the remark of the president that "It takes two to three years to build a mill; we don't try to predict dips which might take place within this period."

The president listed four "types of investments: 1) diversification of product; 2) quality improvement; 3) obsolescence; 4) increased capacity." He added, as "our fundamental philosophy":

We feel that corporations, to be economic units, must 1) give stockholders a return on investments, 2) continue to show gain in working capital, 3) reduce debt, and 4) take care of obsolescence on capital expansion and keep plant and equipment in good shape and in proper position in the industry. No one of these should be subordinated to any of the others.

Capital Expenditure Plans

The president stated that the firm had only a program of approved projects. It had no capital budget other than the approved projects. The controller explained that the firm does have a balance sheet forecast which goes to the board each meeting. (There are five meetings each year.) This forecast includes capital expenditures but seldom goes beyond the end of the next calendar year.

Formal Aspects of Approval

In regard to the procedure for approval of capital expenditures, the president of this container company reported that a management committee made up of the top executives reviews recommended expenditures. Recommendations originate from various sources. The controller added: "We now have an advisory committee which appraises all major improvement plans before they go to management." There are blanket authorizations for certain items under $25,000. An appropriations committee has to approve expenditure coming within this blanket. Every expenditure of more than $25,000 goes to the board of directors for approval. The president declared, "We constantly have much more submitted from our people down the line than either the management committee or the board of directors approves."

Calculations

The president stated the procedure in calculating to ascertain the wisdom of a proposed capital expenditure as follows: take total cost of new asset, apply normal amount of working capital, assume same or reduced profit margin. In 1952, the president explained that anticipated earnings on new assets would have to be as high as actual earnings on the old:

Right now we don't feel justified in recommending new projects which would make less than return on current projects. We would not build new plants which would make less profit than current plants . . . We would compare to the company as a whole. — We're running 15 to 18 per cent on net worth. The project would have to run that high or higher.

Costs of Construction and Equipment

The length of time from approval to completion of expenditure (see next section) makes possible increases in cost considerably beyond estimates, entailing a "31 or 32 per cent deficiency" in the 1946-49 period but only very slight discrepancies later. The president did not see in cost increases a cause of curtailment of expenditures since "where costs go up earnings usually go up." However, he stated, "An increased cushion to allow for increased costs may prevent a proposed project from appearing profitable enough to win approval."

Flexibility and Time Lags

The president reported that the length of time from board approval to completion of a project depends upon the size of the project. This period may be about 15 months for smaller projects, as much as three years for major ones. However, in the 1949 dip, according to the president, while all new projects were held up for 12 months, those in process were not stopped.

The controller stated that the various procedures and time patterns relating to capital expenditures were not inflexible. He explained that one may have a reasonably set program and then something may come along that looks particularly advantageous. "You have to be flexible," he argued, "so that if the complexion changes in a couple of months you can change the program."

Estimates and Surveys

Substantiating the president's assertion that only approved projects were included in the firm's capital expenditure "program" the controller stated, "We don't know at what rate we'll spend appropriations. We think it unsound to forecast the amount we'll spend in a future period." He added that the firm did not fill out information on future commitments on SEC reports "because we don't know."

Firm H (Containers)

This company is a large one in the paper and cardboard container industry. One interview was conducted, involving the president (and treasurer) and the secretary (and controller), with most of the information coming from the former.

A major component of capital expenditures has apparently involved the opening of new plants in the areas to which the firm extended its operations. A frank preference for buying existing facilities, "thus relieving competitor pressure," was expressed but this was not always feasible.

Nature and Extent of Estimates and Plans

Emphasis on long-run growth potentialities and on arranging the strategies and general flexibility which will permit taking advantage of these potentialities as they seem about to be realized is pointed up in the following remarks of the firm's president, early in 1952:

In this business we're *continuously* making changes and expenditures because of new developments and new uses for our product. In the wood business we look pretty far into the future. We thought we had taken care of our needs to perpetuity in lumber. We bought a lot of barren land to make more for 25 years from now. We don't want the people who are running this company in 25 years to say, "What was the matter with those guys in 1950? Didn't they know we were going to grow?"

We have now a capital expenditure project to last through 1953; we're in a second phase, rounding out previous expansion. — We have big expenditures in the offing for rounding out mills. We have many "iffies" — in plants elsewhere. — What will make "iffies" a reality? — It depends on the growth of the business in the area.

Formal Aspects of Approval

The president declared:

All minor expenditures up to $1,000 the men in the plants do themselves. Anything from there on up I approve. The *major* things go to the Board.

We have expenditures in the box plants which keep coming up all the time to keep up with current changes in the picture. Expenditures of $25,000 and $50,000 must have amounted to a million dollars last year.

The Role of Expansion

The president manifested a certain caution in regard to capital expenditures and action on estimates of need for expansion. He explained:

We don't put in a new plant unless the prospects of filling it within four or five years are good. A lot of money and personnel are put into a new plant. We start by putting in a small plant to take care of reasonable growth and then we spread out.

Expansion projects start first, the president pointed out, with converting plants, which prepare the packaging material that meets customer demand. Customer demand, he added, can be influenced by developing new uses. Another step in increasing sales may involve acquiring and utilizing trucks which "can go 400 miles overnight" and "offer local service like having a plant in the community." Then, "when we have expanded our box plants to the ultimate, we expand our mill operation. We do that by revamping . . . Wherever you revamp a paper mill you spend millions of dollars. We always try to get the ultimate out of an old plant before getting a new plant." The general economic situation helps determine the firm's decisions on expanding its own raw material capacity, it is clear. For, the president explained, "If supply exceeds demand we can get materials in the market. But with the war and recent conditions, we have to depend pretty much on our own supplies. What to do? Revamp our own mill!"[36]

---

[36] Commenting on the influence of general business conditions, the president of this large container firm declared:

"It's a funny thing in our company. Usually when business is bad we make our greatest growth (in units produced, not necessarily in sales because prices go down) For instance, when business is bad and a man is packing his material

New Locations

A major element in expansion expenditures is movement into an area where there has been a growth in economic activity. Indicators for expansion are described in these terms: trade area grows, new plants come into an area, and new uses are obtained for the company's products Movement of plants of customers into the South has had a good deal to do with expansion. The following more or less direct quotation of remarks of the president may well summarize how the firm prepares for expansion and how it finally comes to a decision to go ahead:

In the state of . . . for example, business began in . . . in 1927. We took over a plant in . . . and kept expanding it. Our . . . plant has been rebuilt three times. It reached the physical limits of the lot on which it stood and we then bought the lot next door, for which we had to pay a fancy price. Business then expanded in cans for the citrus crops in the southeast. We made a prediction that business would develop greatly in a few years in . . . where we just opened a plant. Actually we own real estate in three or four localities where we know we'll want plants eventually because we see business developing there. We bought properties in the southeast with plans for building all ready but were stymied in building by the war.

Calculations, Depreciation Charges, and Accelerated Amortization

The president declared:

Depreciation charges are no influence. Pay-off periods are calculated on a cash basis whether the cash comes from depreciation or anything else. For example, we are getting a new taping machine that will cost $8,000; it will replace two old ones and will use two people instead of six people. How much will we save? It will save eight months' labor. Therefore there are no further questions about it. It is clearly a worthwhile expenditure.

On the other hand, if we were borrowing money, we would add in all cash savings, including depreciation, to pay off the loan. This is particularly true in regard to "C.N.'s" [government certificates of necessity, authorizing accelerated depreciation, for tax purposes, of assets acquired osten-

---

in wood and metal, we can talk him into paper containers which are cheaper and lighter to ship."

The interviewer at this time explained the "inferior good" proposition of economic theory and the president added:

"Grocery bags are a depression item; more are sold when times are generally bad. Why? When times are good, the housewife buys a whole peck of potatoes in one big bag. When times are bad she makes small purchases and uses a lot of bags."

However, figures published in annual reports showed a 15 to 20 percent drop in net sales in 1949. When the interviewer pointed this out to the president he replied, "We have no set formula on a depression drop."

sibly for production in the interests of national defense]. That makes it [the use of "C.N.'s"] a good deal. We have used "C.N.'s." We have a request in for another one but don't think we'll get it. The government thinks there is enough capacity now in the paper industry. . . . With all the present investigations the government is scared. They're afraid it will be found out that they've given "C.N.'s" to many companies that don't deserve them. But whether we get "C.N.'s" or not we're going ahead anyway.

Calculation of pay-off periods, according to the president, influenced thinking in regard to changes or new equipment but not in regard to new plants. Apparently the rule of thumb in relation to new plant was simply whether its capacity could be expected to be utilized within a few years.

Availability and Cost of Outside Funds

On the question of supply of funds and cost of capital it may be well to quote the president again:

We've never had anything to worry about on that score. We've always had a pretty good backlog of cash. We have available to us now a credit line of [x] million dollars of a long-term debt. Actually we have used only about [35 percent] — We don't like to be in debt. We try to do without frills on our capital expenditure; we don't make any money on a fancy building. . . . The necessity of borrowing money for expansion would not stop us. For example, on a [y] million dollar deal last year we borrowed [55 percent]. We could have paid it off but we have another expansion of ten to twelve million dollars coming up. We're hanging on to [z] million dollars because it's cheap money, 3 per cent money, available for long-term use.

Effect of Taxes

Concerning the effect of taxes, the president said:

Current tax policies reduce borrowing. There are not a lot of new borrowings as you keep only 17¢ or 18¢ of each dollar. Thus if you really need money, you sell securities. . . . With the new tax law, new securities add to the base before excess profits taxes are applied. You do get some help on borrowing but not as much as on new securities.

Flexibility and Time Lags

The president reported that it took two years to get a new building and three to five years (concurrent with the time necessary to acquire a building) to get equipment. Box plants required as much as four to five years.

Whatever the effect of these lags, there was no recent evidence of curtailment of expenditures in the face of declining sales. The president's remarks on this matter were as follows:

If income of business looked bad we would not want to undertake very much. I don't remember curtailing anything though. Of course we wouldn't go ahead on a $10,000,000 paper expansion if we thought the paper industries were going to pot and that we would be able to get all our paper in the market very easily. In 1949 we did not curtail expenditures. They were planned; money had been borrowed and we couldn't stop, so we just went ahead. We would have gone ahead even if things had gone badly. We had a long-term loan (15 years) with cheap money.

Firm I (Shoes)[37]

The president of this firm, which comprises shoe factories, tanneries, warehouses, and sole leather and general supply plants, said: "The shoe industry is a very stable industry. Consumption per capita doesn't change . . . We know the industry's market. It is very stable. It's up to us to capture our share of it."

It should be recalled that a major portion of capital equipment in shoe production is leased and is not owned outright as in most American industries. It is not clear, however, that this causes as great a difference in production of capital equipment for the industry as might be imagined. High surrender costs tend to induce firms to retain equipment once leased and may accordingly make them cautious in the leasing of additional equipment, much as firms generally appear cautious in purchasing capital assets.

On the issue of buying versus leasing equipment, the president explained that some shoe machinery is leased and some is bought but in only a few types can one both buy and lease. "Any machine which we can buy we buy," he declared, "if there is a choice between buying or leasing."

The controller pointed out that dies, lasts, and patterns are recognized as current expenditures by the government and are not listed as capital expenditures. Machinery is purchased by the firm for its tanneries but the bulk of capital expenditures, he stated, was in manufacturing buildings, mainly shoe factories.

Capital Expenditure Plans

The president declared that although "leasing of machinery is a pretty fixed matter," capital expenditure "varies according to needs

---

[37] Three manufacturing firms in the shoe industry were interviewed. They were all "in-stock" houses, that is firms which sell a considerable portion of their product out of stock, beginning production in advance of receipt of orders. Two of these firms manufacture a wide variety of brands and may be referred to as "giant" firms. The third, which is somewhat smaller than the other two, furnished little or no information in regard to capital expenditures; hence, only two firms, I and J, will be included in this report.

and necessities." He insisted, upon some pressing by the interviewer, that the firm "makes no forward plans in capital expenditures" but simply takes "each case as it comes."

Formal Aspects of Approval

In regard to the procedures by which capital expenditures are decided upon and approved, it was learned that the sales managers, who are actually production schedulers in this firm, may stress a need for production beyond current capacity. The manufacturing department then comes to the executive committee to prove the need for new expenditures. The president denied making any "distinction between replacement, expansion in old products, and expansion in new products in regard to criteria for approving capital purchases."

The Role of Expansion

The now familiar concern for definite and long-run expectations of increases in demand before capacity is expanded is indicated by the following statements by the firm's president:

We would have to have pretty definite expectations before we leased or bought additional machines. — How would you get these "definite expectations"? — We watch the trend of the market.
We build new plant or capacity when sales are running greater than capacity and there are sufficient new accounts to justify additional capacity. We have capacity on a full five day week of [x] thousand a day. We might not authorize a new capital expenditure until we had produced up to schedule, "tight" for a year. . . . We might just refuse to deliver a line in short supply if expansion did not seem warranted. . . . We might shift one brand to another factory if a shortage seemed temporary. If the shortage seemed permanent we might have to get a new plant.

The controller declared, in another interview, "Generally speaking we're operating our factories at 98 percent of capacity now; getting more shoes means getting them from additional factories. On a new factory — be darned sure for it will cost a lot."

The president summarized well the expressions on the matter heard by the interviewer in this firm with the statement: "Before capacity expansion we have to determine whether a shortage is permanent or temporary — perhaps it's just a fad — and whether other capacity is available which might be utilized to meet the shortage."

Capital Supply Considerations

The president of the firm minimized the significance of cost of capital and construction in determining the volume of the firm's capital expenditures. On costs of construction he said:

We're building an office building probably at the top of the market now. . . . We make capital expenditures when we need them. . . . We are considering building warehouses on the railroad tracks. We must decide just how to distribute them. Surveys are still being made. Costs and the problem of borrowing money are not what is holding us up.

On the cost of money the president said:

We're not influenced by the cost of money. We won't put in a new plant unless demand warrants it. Financing is mostly from internal sources. . . . We have borrowed money and incurred debt in securing additional working capital, not for capital expenditures.

Asked whether the firm would borrow money for a potentially profitable capital expenditure if internal funds were not available for it, the president replied, smiling, "Sure we would, if it would make money." To this the controller rejoined, also smiling, "You'd have to be sure though, wouldn't you?"

Accuracy of Estimates and Reaction to Surveys

The controller offered some information on how he handled Commerce-SEC capital expenditure questionnaires received by his firm. He declared that he included in anticipated expenditures only those projects definitely planned; he would not anticipate any expenditures which were not known. He claimed that "on the short period we are very accurate, except for going over from one quarter to the next because the builder didn't complete the job on time. When we get the bill is when we put the expenditure on the books." A discrepancy between planned and actual expenditures in the third quarter of 1951 (when planned expenditures for new plant were only a little over 70 percent of actual expenditures) was explained with the statement, "This balanced out the discrepancy of the previous quarter."

In determining the amount of planned expenditures the controller reported writing to the firm's engineer and purchasing agents for estimates. However, the practice of listing only those future expenditures definitely planned would tend, he felt, to cause greater underestimates where the period under consideration was further in the future.

Firm J (Shoes)

This firm owns shoe factories, sole cutting and shoe supply plants, warehouses, and tanneries in at least nine states. A number of officials were interviewed but major information in regard to capital expenditures was obtained from the controller.

An apparently dominant characteristic is the recognized long-term steady growth of the industry. The company was reported to have held just over a certain percentage of the industry's sales for many years. Thus it shared in a "gradual change to a larger volume of shoes," in an industry which was viewed as a "level proposition," because of its fairly constant growth.

In addition to the growth in over-all output, it was pointed out that more factories were needed now than formerly for given outputs because of the increase in diversification. More warehouses were needed, for example, to handle greater varieties of sizes and styles. There are now 10 times as many items, it was explained, as there were twenty-five years ago.

Nature of Plans and Formal Aspects of Approval

The controller declared that his firm had no "long-run capital expenditure plans." The nature of capital expenditure plans may perhaps be illustrated by the following example.

In one instance a director became concerned about the number of shoes the company was producing with outside manufacturers' nationally advertised heels. Simultaneously, the director in charge of supplies was concerned with the lack of orders for the company's own leather tanning plants. Thus a man was hired to study combinations of plastic and rubber. It was hoped that chemical research would show the company a way to do the job, making optimum use of its own facilities.

Before engineers go to work laying out a plant, it was explained, the company wants to be sure it can make successfully the materials to be produced. The company wants to perfect its knowledge first, not to proceed by "trial and error." When this knowledge is acquired the engineers go ahead and lay out the plant. The industrial managers pick the site. Costs are calculated. The financial department decides where the money is coming from. But all money spent at this time pays for exploratory work.

Then the engineers will sketch out the area. Names of the necessary machines will be ascertained by management. Outside suppliers will be contacted. Finally management will get to the point of saying: this is it — amount, cost, projected profit, and so on. Then the matter is taken to the board of directors for approval.

It is still subject to cancellation for a short period, in the event of a business downturn such as the Great Depression. However, it is progressively harder to cancel as commitments are made to suppliers. The general manager has already outlined plans. He already has the nod of approval from a small group of top officials. Thus he has the approval to go ahead, subject to continuance of the conditions on which the approval is based.

The Roles of Expansion and New Products

Need of additional plant and equipment is occasioned frequently by product innovation. However, expansions into new products (new types of shoes) do not always necessitate much in the way of capital expenditures because of the widespread existence of surplus capacity in the form of idle plants which can be activated with relatively minor expenditures.

The fashion in which the firm introduced a new shoe offered further evidence of the concern felt lest expansion be undertaken improperly on the basis of a merely temporary increase in demand. In one case under current consideration it was related that merely by describing a new shoe on the telephone, the company was able to secure orders for 100,000 pairs. But then manufacturing difficulties developed and orders were refused on all new accounts. Finally, it was decided to open a new factory to produce the shoe. The possibility was recognized that "it could be just one of those flashy things." But in this case the conviction was reached that this was not so, that rather it represented "a new trend."

Expansion and Cost Reduction

A curious illustration of the relation between expansion of capacity and reduction of costs is involved in the practice of maintaining idle plants which are activated when needed. This enables the company, in the face of changing relative costs, to concentrate production in those plants where operating costs are lowest. Thus, it was explained, the company built new, modern one-floor factories after the war and equipped them. This was a relatively big expansion. The new plants were found to be efficient and capacity was in excess of demand. The company did not, in fact, expect to use all of the capacity it created. But there were various local problems which would affect costs in different areas. The shoe industry is "very competitive." It was felt that one could be in the best possible competitive position, cost-wise, by building this large number of plants after the war and hence securing the freedom to meet local high-cost situations with the possibility of alternative facilities.

A type of local cost increase resulting in a move from a high-cost area was revealed in the example of a community in which a new armament plant bid up labor costs. An example of activation of idle plant as a means of meeting expanded demand relates to the new shoe just described. In this case, it was explained, basic shoe machinery would be acquired from the United Shoe Machine Company. Other shoe machinery had been stored. To activate the plant would involve a cost of $175,000 in the ensuing sixty-day period. It was estimated that $100,000 of this amount would consist of actual property additions.

It was explained that this sort of shifting of plant and equipment and reactivation of idle plants is a source of continual expenditure, usually involving some property additions. These expenditures have been coming out of the "dollar depreciation allowances." Thus one function of capital expenditures for *expansion,* as undertaken in the postwar period, was to provide an adequate distribution of surplus capacity to permit *cost reduction* by the relatively minor expenditures (out of depreciation charges) incident to shifting production from one plant to another.

Firm K (Rubber)[38]

Nature and Extent of Estimates and Plans

The head of market analysis of this rubber and tire firm, in his letter answering the interviewer's summary questions on the role of expectations, wrote:

Decisions regarding capital expenditures and capital requirements invariably are based on estimates as to future prospects. The probable trend of demand for a specific product or for a class of products, or of demand in a specific area and of the probable profits are, in the final analysis, the foundation for any decision as to what we will make, how much capacity we will build, where we will build it, and how and where we will distribute what we do make.

Forecasting in the rubber and tire industry is carried on in a fairly sophisticated and rather similar fashion in all of the firms interviewed. Directors of economic and statistical research of a large number of firms in the industry, including all of the big four, meet quarterly under the auspices of the Rubber Manufacturers' Association and compare and pool forecasts of the demand for tires in the industry. Forecasts are based on a variety of factors, including information on population, income, vehicle registrations, and the like. Separate projections are made for "original equipment" (the tires sold with new cars), "replacement," and export as well as for numerous other categories of

---

[38] Firms K, L, M, and N constitute the "big four" of the rubber and tire industry. Where officers interviewed have unique titles, these titles have been modified in the accounts which follow, to avoid revealing the identities of their firms.

sales. These industry forecasts have been made available to the interviewer and will, it is hoped, eventually be subjected to statistical analysis. However, the firms' anticipations of their own sales are closely guarded secrets.

The head of market analysis declared that the sales department determines what percentage of the industry total the firm can expect to receive. The final estimate is a top management decision. This figure is compared with current capacity to determine what expansion is necessary.

Forecasts of future sales generally run to five years in length. However, 10-year forecasts are also utilized and are justified, according to the head of market analysis, in order "to know what will happen to agricultural rubber. Agricultural products take at least seven years to expand capacity, by means of new plantings." The 10-year forecasts are also useful because "it takes a long time to pay off facilities." The head of market analysis stated as his principle: "Be confident of your forecast. Don't be afraid to be wrong. Don't revise your forecast for temporary changes, for example, dealer inventory accumulation because of price increases of crude rubber on the world market."

Although forecasts of sales run ahead many years, capital expenditures are usually forecast for three to four years.

Formal Aspects of Approval

It was reported that the detailed engineering design and estimated cost of projects are prepared by the Engineering Department in conjunction with production staff personnel. If the project contemplates cost reduction or will increase capacity and income, then the cost accounting division with the help of the process engineer, and time study and sales divisions, depending on the project, must compute savings or additional income to be realized.

The production superintendent submits complete detailed estimates to the vice-president in charge of production. The vice-president in charge of production reviews and forwards these estimates to the plant accountant for further analysis and comments. The plant accountant forwards them to the president of the division, with his comments. After his approval, it is reviewed by the treasurer with the plant accountant prior to submission to the "Appropriation Council" for approval. Larger projects require executive committee or even board approval.

The Role of Expansion

In regard to the usual emphasis on the significance of sales and demand, one official said, "There should be a certain relationship between additional property expenditure and sales volume. If we spend we should get sales."

Calculations

For projects that do not claim savings or additional income (replacement, quality improvement, and so forth) the proposed expenditure is compared with the best alternative to determine the advisability of making such expenditure. For instance, the cost of replacing a unit would be compared with the cost of overhauling and continuing its use, or if feasible, compared with the cost of having work done on the outside. A project for quality improvement would be compared with what would result if the expenditure were not made.

On projects claiming cost reduction or additional income, it was reported that the company deducts interest and depreciation from the savings and computes net savings or additional income after Federal income taxes. To determine the "payback period," depreciation is added back to the net savings figure.

Capital Supply Considerations

The cash forecast was reported to be a "very important projection." It was explained that this forecast determines if the company will have to do some additional financing or reduce expansions contemplated. It also influences dividend policy. All present expansion of facilities, one of the respondents adds, has been financed out of earnings.

Flexibility

This company adjusts its plan quickly if the economic conditions change, a financial officer reported. Substantiating the above, he noted that capital expenditures projected for 1949 were some 25 percent above what was actually spent in that recession year.

Firm L (Rubber)

Nature and Extent of Estimates and Plans

Emphasizing the need for long-run forecasts, the statistician of this rubber and tire company said:

We have spent $100 million in the last couple of years on capital [expenditures] and improvements, based on forecasts of the future. You can't expand now for the present or even for 1953 [the next year] . . . . In building plant now we want to know about 1956 or 1957 requirements. There's no use building a plant for 1954 and getting just one year of production.

However, the financial vice-president said that although there was a postwar committee at the end of the war looking into the future, the firm has "no five-year capital expenditure plans. If you talk to the vice president in charge of development and research, you'd find he has various things in mind but many will never come to fruit; it will depend on conditions. Planning too far ahead just gets asinine." By way of buttressing this point, the financial vice-president explained: "We don't respond to [a national survey of capital expenditure plans]. They want us to forecast things we don't have."

An assistant controller explained:

Each year there is a master budget indicating the projects to come up that year, prepared at the beginning of each year. It is really a combination of estimates of commitments (outside) and expenditures (the company's own labor). This is seldom completely spent during the year; it is just an estimate of what is to be started.

Formal Aspects of Approval

The financial vice-president explained some of the procedures by which capital expenditures are determined as follows:

Basically we operate under a master budget which starts with capital expenditures. Early in the fall people concerned start working on it. We divide it into normal replacement and expansion. This is prepared by the departments. The master budget is a plan, not an authorization of expenditures. Items are classified as replacement and expansion.

The other side is the expense budget. [A master budget involves no approval of expenditures; approval is monthly in specific budgets.] There are also emergency budgets capable of action at any time. There are additions and transfers through the year. No capital budgets are good for more than 90 days. Long-term expenditures are carried on an annual basis. Incomplete projects go into "unliquidated budgets." Of $50,000,000 of unliquidated expenditures in a budget, $20,000,000 may be commitments to outsiders, some of which may be cancelled if the 90 day period from approval to commitment, not necessarily payment, which will take some time longer, is expired.

Capital expenditures, approved and proposed, are listed by this company in what is known as a "blue book," given to directors several times a year upon the occasion of revisions. According to the financial vice-president, again, listings in the blue book are broken into:

1. Total of approved projects only.
2. Projects coming during the year [not yet approved].
3. Projects under active consideration for the future.

The Role of Expansion

The assistant controller declared, "The development [of new products] phase is another story altogether. Development is a part of research, leading to business for we don't know how far in the future." New products apparently offer a particularly large field for expansion in the rubber and allied products industry, with major tire companies active in the production of synthetic fibers and a large variety of rubber products. In more than one firm reference was made to the possibility of utilizing rubber in the construction of highways, a development that would bring a huge increase in the aggregate demand for rubber.

One interesting example may be noted of a capital expenditure contemplated by the firm (in response to expectations of sales and desire to maintain share of market) which would not increase aggregate investment. This contemplated expenditure is the purchase from the government of a synthetic rubber plant when the government gives it up.

The Role of Replacement

The financial vice-president declared: "The Board doesn't look at replacement budgets at all. Departments decide replacement." However, at another point he remarked:

Even small replacements are accompanied by studies to show how long it will take to pay for expenditures. Now with taxes we can't use that yardstick.
. . . . .

An economic reaction might lead to tightening of replacement expenditures; for example, painting of cotton mills, which is a big operation, can be put off.

Capital Supply Considerations

The financial vice-president, as might be expected, had a good bit to say about sources of funds. According to him capital expenditures that are approved become "outstanding capital commitments." He added:

Our *own* accounts (not outside) always provide for liquidation of these commitments. Our interior accounts thus show a true working capital picture. U. S. Steel Company does it with cash. They must be well supplied with cash. . .

Since 1946, U. S. business has expanded more than ever before without ever making financial provision in advance. In the last six years we, like the rest of them, have expanded like the devil. . . Twice in the post-war years we have borrowed in [x] million dollar loans. We just made one last [name of month]. It was just an accident that we came to this just before the money market tightened up and rates went up. . . . We're one of the minority of companies that got funds first. Last March I argued that after taxes and supporting dividends we would not have enough to finance our expansion. Hence we couldn't have a sinking fund.

We have not had to be influenced by availability of funds on capital expenditure plans in domestic business. Abroad it has been a consideration as we've been reluctant to send new dollars abroad. Foreign expansion depended on their ability to get funds.

Taxes and the Rate of Interest

The financial vice-president stated:

The killing of capital markets, which started with Roosevelt, makes us borrow privately. Actually taxes reduce the cost of borrowing money. We actually gained $134,000 by borrowing. For by provisions of the Revenue Act, by borrowing money you get an extra 9 per cent on your excess profits. Of course, we'd have to maintain high profits to keep this.

He reported further that:

We got 3½ per cent on our second loan. Our first loan in the fall of . . . was 2¾ and 3 per cent. The impact of higher rates would be very slight after taxes. The rate was the only thing I did not negotiate. The rate was the least of my considerations. Ordinarily it could never amount to much . . . I negotiated other terms; the no-sinking provision was very important.

One may infer that a supply of *long-term* funds is of particular significance. Sinking funds, one would presume, reduce the effective average duration of loans.

Accelerated Amortization

The financial vice-president was enthusiastic about the value of accelerated depreciation:

We've applied vigorously for certificates of necessity but are not doing too well with the government. . . . We haven't gotten more than 25 per cent of the C.N.'s we've asked for . . . The present C.N.'s are not as good as during the war. They are now only applicable to 30 to 60 per cent of each capital expenditure.

During the last war it was almost a racket. We got a lot of free assets. We were the first one to get up a form and got our applications approved relatively easily because they were on forms.

Flexibility and Time Lags

The firm's statistician commented on lags between decisions and expenditures and on opportunities to make expenditures substantially different in amount from those originally decided upon. He declared:

It takes two or three or four months before executives can . . . make a final decision. For example, now they want a new review of facts, long-run forecasts, etc. That takes us time and then it takes time for the Board of Directors to approve; it may take six months. Then, if we had it approved and decided today, it would be the fourth quarter before we could get steel and get started. — There might be a delay in getting money from banks, and the like. Then, of course, construction takes much longer now than years ago. The [x] Company, with a monopoly on big presses, is filled up through 1953 and we probably could not get anything from them until 1954.

The financial vice-president reported, on the matter of adjustment to changing patterns of demand:

Whether projects are carried through in the face of adverse developments is based on how far advanced — how much cost — and where it could be used elsewhere. We check with sales and see how persuasive sales people can be as to the picture six months from now and a year from now.

. . . . .

The present total of unliquidated projects includes nothing further ahead than 2½ years. . . . If there is a business drop these may mature very quickly as suppliers lose other sales and hence supply ahead of schedule those customers who have not cancelled.

It is interesting to note that this last point might mean that an observer of *ex post* statistics would find that the early effects of a decline in business conditions might appear quite mixed. While some firms would be canceling expenditures others would be accelerating them.

Firm M (Rubber)
Nature and Extent of Estimates and Plans

Like other rubber and tire companies, Firm M is greatly concerned with future trends in its still rapidly growing and developing industry. In answer to our "summary questions" on expectations the financial vice-president wrote:

The most obvious need for looking ahead relates to the matter of being sure we will have adequate facilities to meet the estimated forward demand for our products. Here we try to look at least three to five years ahead. Estimation of permanent new capital requirements is also related to our expectations of future trends of a long-term nature.

The firm economist added in subsequent (1955) discussion of this point that his economics department was always working ahead five or six years in future estimates. Various forecasts went ahead ten or twelve years as seemed appropriate. Among the variables whose magnitudes were forecast one year ahead (by quarters) by the economics department and reported upon for three past years (twelve quarters) were industrial production, personal income, disposable personal income, "disposable personal income above essentials" (explained as the best indicator of demand for certain of the company's products), department store sales, retail sales of automotive parts and accessories and of household appliances and radios, production of automobiles and trucks (including output for the military), industry tire shipments (broken down into passenger car, truck, and farm categories), and United States rubber consumption in long tons. The economist seemed to have a well-developed technique of utilizing major current indexes and statistics in arriving at his estimates. He indicated that he watched closely all of the big industries, including government, which were important to cyclical fluctuations.

In relation to capital expenditures for purposes of expanding capacity, the financial vice-president said, "We want to prepare for the expected peak." The economist explained that the firm wanted to have ample capacity to handle "peak loads" in the manner of utilities. The firm "wants to build five or six or seven years ahead. We like to have a certain margin over the peak load. When this margin is reduced we have to think about plant expansion. It is this relation [between peak load and capacity] which determines the big capital expenditures."

Problems of the timing of contemplated expenditures are such that the firm does not find it appropriate to have formal long-range capital budgets which specify the amounts and types of capital expenditures by year over, for example, a five-year period. Actual forward budgeting may go ahead about two years and is likely to involve only plans for the completion of currently approved projects. The pace of expenditures on approved projects is suggested by the financial vice-president's statement, "We would go ahead as quickly as we could physically." An important factor in the timing of capital expenditures is apparently the supply of management services available to the company as well as the delays incident to making appropriate arrangements with outside suppliers, governmental authorities, and others who may be concerned.

The absence of formal capital budgets which go ahead a number of years on an annual basis should not be taken to indicate a lack of forward planning of capital expenditures, it was explained. The financial vice-president declared: "Long-range programs are talked about all the time. They finally get to the executive committee when ready to get approval for money. . . . There is no long-run program prior to approval *in a formal sense.*" He explained further that even though the company did not have long-range expenditure plans in the "sense of actually appropriating, we know what we'll do."

Formal Aspects of Approval

Appropriations of $15,000 or more, the financial vice-president explained, must come to the executive committee, which consists of six of the company's directors. The vice-president in charge of production and the financial vice-president can jointly approve expenditures up to $15,000.

The financial vice-president referred to the monthly "plant investment and executive committee appropriations" report as "our bible." This report includes unspent appropriations carried over from the previous year as well as current-year appropriations. It also includes a comparison of the total of plant expenditures of the current year with such expenditures for the same months of the previous year.

The controller's office has the task of ascertaining the financial needs implicit in the company's demand for new plant and equipment. In performing this task it considers "all projects that factories have in mind for the current year that they want to do." These projects are classified in the categories of expansion, improvement, or replacement. Explaining further the development of capital expenditure estimates and their path to approval and execution, the controller declared:

> The vice-president in charge of production decides where production will be put. The plant expenditure estimate comes from the engineering department. Things are in a mental stage for a while. The engineering department makes up a work order for each of these projects. They are approved by the executive committee. . . . When approved, the expenditure can be counted and added to previous approvals. If we have approved an order on which the plants have not gone ahead for a year or so, we can cancel it out and then they come in again [for approval].

The Role of Expansion

In explaining long-run demand forecasts the company economist declared, "We can always add another 5 per cent on capacity. We can't add 40 per cent." It seems reasonable to read into this remark the implication that minor fluctuations in demand would be met without capital expansion. This was confirmed by later discussion (1955) when the economist explained that minor increases in demand can be handled by overtime work, working an extra day in the week, building inventories in slack seasons, and by "small modest outlays" which involve some "improvising" or improvement in "ways of doing things" which expand capacity.

However, it was clear that the company anticipated a major growth in demand which would have to be met by major capital expenditures. The financial vice-president said: "We have a marvelous growth coming. Everything is on rubber. Real growth is also coming abroad." As discussed earlier, company policy was directed toward being prepared in advance to meet the expected peaks in demand.

Expansion did not mean, necessarily, acquisition of new plant. The financial vice-president explained that management had to decide the "problem of new plant versus expansion of old plant. . . . We discuss in executive committee whether we should have another tire factory or expand present tire facilities." Similarly, in regard to facilities for a proposed new product, he remarked: "We've never been in ———. We talk about it. We have not yet decided whether to build a new plant or take over some present plant." The company economist indicated that factors militating in favor of expanding existing plants were the existence of various "utilities" such as power plants, repair facilities, and machine shops, which frequently have a reserve capacity to handle greater production in the existing plant, but which would have to be duplicated in a new plant. Factors in favor of a plant in a new location would include such items as superior labor supply and warehouse facilities.

How a firm actually meets an increase in demand — by acquiring an existing plant of another firm, expanding existing plant, or building a new plant — is, of course, of great significance for the aggregate of investment in the economy. The opportunity to choose among these alternatives, at the firm level, suggests a need for care and caution in translating data on investment and capacity obtained by survey techniques, from individual firms, to corresponding variables for the economy as a whole.

The Role of Replacement

It was clear that "replacement" typically involved improvement of plant and equipment and consequently expansion. The financial vice-president said:

In the ordinary run of business new improvements are always coming in. We have new facilities coming in on a going basis over a three to four year period. We'll have a program of building new machines to change over a certain kind of tire building. A lot of improved machines may reduce the required floor space and hence reduce the number of new plants required.[39]

We are replacing equipment with better equipment. Two years ago we saw this coming and started a building program at [X] and improvements elsewhere. [X] was one of our smaller factories — good labor market, fine labor relations, land, good markets. . . .

---

[39] Capital-saving innovation?

The company economist declared, "Every time we replace equipment we add to potential capacity, because the new equipment is more productive. An increase of capacity of some facilities in this manner may induce expansion in other complementary facilities." Thus, a sharp line of distinction between expenditures for replacement, improvement, and expansion, while frequently a useful, if crude, tool for operating executives as well as economic analysts, cannot be taken correctly as the basis for mutually exclusive economic categories. As just indicated, replacement, improvement, locational factors, and expansion are all intermeshed.

Calculations

On the subject of calculations to ascertain the wisdom of capital expenditures, the financial vice-president declared:

The vice-president in charge of production will write up an engineering department request for an appropriation. It will give complete information to justify the request and, in addition, will show the years to pay off, after taxes . . . The pay-off period is important in such matters. Current and prospective tax rates also weigh heavily in the larger expenditures. For example, we might undertake a new powerhouse later when increased profits from lower costs would not be 82 per cent taxed away.

Capital Supply Considerations

The financial vice-president stated the company position as follows: "If we decide to go ahead on a project, we'll get the money from profits or new capital." Although conversations with the controller may give the impression that funds immediately available represent an important constraint ("You can only spend what you've got"), it appears rather that the controller's function in these matters is to see that expenditures are in line with what has been approved.

Accelerated Amortization

Concerning accelerated depreciation for tax purposes, such as was available (even before passage of the Internal Revenue Code of 1954, which permitted new, generally accelerated forms of depreciation for tax purposes) by means of certificates of necessity for facilities alleged to be necessary in the interests of national defense, the financial vice-president said:

A fast write-off is an inducement to go ahead. But now [1952] you get a certificate of necessity on only 30 to 60 per cent of value. But that is not always decisive. For example, on a cotton mill in the south, we're trying to get a certificate of necessity, but we'll go ahead whether we get it or not.

The company economist added in 1955 that where basic capacity requirements and expansion were concerned, he felt that certificates of necessity did not weigh too heavily; "they might speed up expenditures a bit."

Flexibility and Time Lags

The company economist indicated that lags of considerable magnitude occurred frequently from the time capital expenditure decisions were made until the expenditures were carried out, simply because of the period necessary for management to make arrangements. In some instances deliveries of equipment furnished by a certain single supplier were lagging a couple of years behind orders. In some cases the company will proceed cautiously in making a series of expenditures of a particular nature, testing for results of its first expenditures before going further. Thus the financial vice-president described a project proposed for one of the firm's plants. "We think it is fine; we'll have it approved there and see how it works out. This may be $7,000,000 there [in the first plant] and $4,000,000 elsewhere if it is carried through."

In regard to responses to changes in the business situation, the firm economist said, "On capital expenditures management can change their mind fast, depending upon how they look at the business picture." However, in 1955, the economist explained that the business picture would influence the timing of capital expenditures in the short run rather than its long-run total. A fall in economic activity would slow up capital expenditure, but even here the effect might not be immediate since it does not pay to "build a plant half way and then stop."

The financial vice-president said:

If we had a definite change in the economy we'd take a good look at conditions. We would look at all phases — inventories, expenses, personnel — not just capital expenditures ... I was around in 1920 when sales suddenly stopped ... We owed millions of dollars to banks and had large inventories. Prices were immediately reduced very substantially to quickly provide funds to reduce our large bank loans. All expenses were curtailed, and of necessity, employees were temporarily laid off. And in 1937 there were two wage cuts, when sales dropped off following President Roosevelt's declaration that there was too much inventory.

Firm N (Rubber)

The president and the financial vice-president of this rubber and tire company fitted their remarks on capital expenditures of the firm at least in part into the financial classification of capital expenditures used in the company. This classification is presented here as stated in a firm document (hereafter referred to as "Document A") made available to the interviewer:

Class I — Expenditures essential to continue operations and maintain satisfactory quality — This class shall embrace expenditures for plants, equipment and facilities and the maintenance thereof as required to produce goods of satisfactory quality, style and design.

Class II — Expenditures involving economies in operations — This class shall embrace expenditures for equipment and facilities that will result in lower manufacturing costs — usually termed savings. It is intended to be used to acquire equipment of improved design or to provide funds for the rearrangement of plant, with the object of reducing manufacturing costs.

Class III — Expenditures incidental to expanding existing production — This class shall embrace equipment and/or change in facilities that will result in expanding existing production.

Class IV — Expenditures incidental to introducing new products or entering a new business — This class shall embrace expenditures for equipment required for the initial commercial production of new products. New products include any item which is not currently being produced. It shall also include expenditures for equipment transferred from development for use in the manufacture of new products.

Nature and Extent of Estimates and Plans

The following rather extensive quotation from the answer to "summary questions" by the company president offers a useful background and context for more specific comments made in the course of the interviews with this firm:

As a company, we operate on a decentralized basis. The operating divisions participate in several industries with characteristics and trends peculiar to that particular business. Accordingly, the future of the company is the reflection of the future projects of these decentralized divisional operations.

There are two ways in which advice with respect to general economics becomes available to the divisional management. Our Commercial Research Department is equipped with economic data and is prepared to express the general thinking of company management with respect to future trends.[40]

---

[40] An officer of the company, commenting on this, wrote to this interviewer:

"The first half of this sentence is correct, but the last half must depend on interpretation Actually our Commercial Research furnishes economic data to the various operating departments but as a preliminary step it is not their function to express management thinking that comes after consideration of economic and other data by the Executive Committee and the General Managers, followed by joint discussions by the two groups. To understand this, the uninformed reader may have to wait until he reads the complete page, and particularly the last sentence which reads 'Our final decision on company policy reflects the thinking of the group' (Executive Committee and General Managers)."

Also, we retain the services of an outside economist who meets with our management each month. In addition each division maintains a statistical staff relating to the particular industries in which it operates. This staff work is reflected in the forward projections of sales, profits, investment, and return on investment at the level of the General Manager of the operating division. Forecasts are regularly made one year ahead and from time to time divisions are requested for broad estimates extending over longer periods.

Each division submits these forward projections to the Executive Committee. When approved, they become the plan of operation and all business decisions with respect to the affairs of that division are made against this background. Such business decisions would involve approval of major capital expenditures, consideration of expansions in existing products or new ventures — in fact, all of the major decisions of policy on which decision is required from the Executive Committee.

As an individual I do have expectations and personal points of view. I get them from daily contacts with the staff, general reading, discussions with my associates, and from conversations with my friends and business acquaintances outside of the company. However, my personal views do not determine company policy. Such policies are usually based on recommendations which come up through the organization. These proposals are approved or changed in the Executive Committee, where my own views are subjected to the same discussions and considerations as those of any other member. Our final decisions on company policy reflect the thinking of the group.

In regard to the use of long-run forecasts, the statistician in the treasurer's office remarked: "The long-range forecast is maintained all the time but at many times is not important. Then when you approach capacity you find long-range forecasts are important." It seems reasonable to infer that long-run forecasts are important when they indicate demand at or in excess of capacity because they then point to the necessity of initiating capital expenditures in order to expand capacity.

The assistant treasurer, in correspondence with the interviewer, ascribed variations in the length of forward capital expenditure estimates to capital supply considerations, explaining that "forward cash requirements planning for several years . . . would of course require data on capital expenditures beyond one year. . . ." He also declared, "Our forward plans for capital expenditures vary . . . Currently [December, 1954] we are completing our plans for capital expenditures for the full year 1955. Last year our plans were also limited to one year, but for about five years preceding 1954 they varied for periods from two to five years." He wrote, further:

In answer to the question "what circumstances would bring about such differences": The best example we can give is to go back about five years, when there were indications that additional working capital and plant facilities would be required for expanded business. It seemed apparent we had to know our forward cash needs. During that period, similar to other companies, we were planning increases in our long-term debt, and the reasons therefor and amount thereof had to be defined. Obviously, our thinking as to capital expenditures over the succeeding five years became very important. . . .

Capital expenditure plans are necessary in order to properly control cash. . . .

In reply to a question as to the extent that plans involved "strategies" for various contingencies the assistant controller wrote:

We do not have "contingent" plans as such, but not infrequently our operating divisions have tentative projects that are being considered subject to more definite consideration of the project after the tentative plans have been more fully developed. Specifically, we had tentative plans for the erection of a new central general laboratory for a period of three to four years before the approved plan was finally accepted in principle. This latter did not become a definite part of our forward plans until it had been so approved by the Executive Committee.

The amount of detail in the capital expenditure plans depends upon the size of projects and their imminence. Thus, for one- and two-year plans, the assistant treasurer explains, ". . . The approved budgets are supported by schedules of individually detailed projects for all expenditures over $25,000. Projects totaling up to $5,000 are summarized by plants, without details, and projects involving expenditures of $5,000 to $25,000 are individually listed but require only limited details." Forecasts beyond two years, although involving estimates "in conjunction with the operating divisions," are "done top side," and do "not get into similar details as is required for the one and two year budgets. In other words, budgets for the first and second years are on a formal basis; those going beyond the second year are less formal."

Formal Aspects of Approval

Document A states: "The final responsibility for the development of a request for plant expenditures rests with the General Manager and Department Head in charge of the division or department requesting the expenditures."

Under a subsection labeled "authority" it indicates "the level of authority to which the request must be submitted for final approval" as follows:

	Class I	Class II	Class III	Class IV
Not exceeding $5,000	General Manager or Department Head	General Manager or Department Head	General Manager or Department Head	Executive Committee
$5,001 to $25,000	Director of Engineering	Director of Engineering	Director of Engineering	Executive Committee
$25,001 to $300,000	Executive Committee	Executive Committee	Executive Committee	Executive Committee
Over $300,000	Finance Committee	Finance Committee	Finance Committee	Finance Committee

The General Managers, Department Heads, and Director of Engineering can delegate authority to their respective assistants to approve appropriation requests in their absence.

A letter addressed to the Executive Committee written by the General Manager or Department Head shall accompany each copy of appropriation requests over $300,000, outlining the purpose, scope and financial aspects of the project.

The Role of Replacement

Even Class I expenditures (essential to continue operations and maintain satisfactory quality), we learn from the president, include "big jobs like revamping of a power plant, which can be put off for a year or two years." Generally, however, Class I expenditures vary "with age of equipment and obsolescence of equipment" and lend themselves "to some readiness in forecasting."

Calculations

Considerable detailed information is available from this firm on criteria for capital expenditures. It is interesting to note how rules of thumb which in themselves would appear irrational in certain situations are modified by other rules of thumb with no explicit indication that the underlying economic principles are being accounted for. Thus, depreciation costs on new investment are included as part of "cost of sales" in estimation of expected rates of profit on prospective investments.

However, including depreciation costs and calculating the "rate of annual return" as the relevant figure, regardless of how long the asset will last,[41] introduces a distinct bias into the estimates, in favor of both

---

[41] On Class II expenditures (involving economies in operation) and on Class III expenditures (for expansion) "the rate of annual returns" is calculated on the basis of expectations for the first two years of operation whereas on Class IV expenditures (for new products) calculations are tied to the first *three* years However, this is a matter of making allowance for the longer time which may be required to develop and sell a new product. Calculations still involve an average annual rate rather than a sum of expected returns.

long-lived and extremely short-lived assets.[42] No clear awareness of this was evidenced in the firm. But it is to be noted that the document referred to earlier states, with reference both to Class III and to Class IV expenditures (expansion and new products):

> The Executive Committee will expect a return on the total of new investment of not less than 25 per cent when the total amount of the appropriation request is over $300,000, and of not less than 50 per cent when the total amount of the appropriation request is $300,000 or less.

Now if one were to make the assumption — confirmed in a later visit to the firm — that the more expensive projects were generally rather long-lived plant expenditures, it would appear that the differentiated requirement in accordance with amount of appropriation may actually add a further weight in favor of long-term projects. Apparently, the company finds it desirable to have a set of criteria for investment projects which prevent the expenditure program from being dominated by short-term, high-profit, fast-turnover ventures.

It is important to realize that probably the most interesting and important aspect of rules of thumb is the circumstances under which they are violated or modified. In discussing Class II expenditures (involving economies in operations), the president of the firm said:

> It all depends on how tight you are and on how much return you wanted. It is now 50 per cent. It has been 25 per cent and 100 per cent. In the 1930's with the depression we had to have 100 per cent. That was based on bad financial condition and the company reputation in the 20's and 30's. From 1936 to 1939 on, on a 25 per cent return we realized there was a lot to be done.[43]

---

[42] See pp. 29-34

[43] In answer to a question in regard to the 50 percent versus the 25 percent criterion, submitted along with a draft of this section, an officer of the firm wrote: "Reference to your question as to why a return of 50% is required on appropriation requests of less than $300,000, but only 25% on requests of more than $300,000: Here we are referring to Class III and Class IV projects only . The general reason for the 50 vs. 25% is — generally the appropriations involving higher amounts are considered of a more stable nature and pertain to activities which it is felt will have a long life, and are of a nature that over a fairly long period will work out to full advantage. Experience has shown that expenditures for the smaller amount quite frequently are short lived and not of the merit of appropriations for the higher amount. Sometimes we approve appropriations for an amount under the $300,000 mark on the basis of a return of less than 50%, depending on the nature of the project and the circumstances surrounding it, all of which would be fully explained in a letter accompanying the appropriation request. As explained during your visit, these rules — including recommended return on investment — are subject to change, and are generally set to suit circumstances and conditions known (or that may be expected) at the time the rules are set. In other words, although the rules are generally closely followed, there can be deviations for cause."

To this the finance chairman added: "You have to admit it depends pretty much on the economic atmosphere. Right now we're in a tight spot. We think it's good to tighten up now. We may be heading into rough seas."

On the Class II expenditures (involving economies in operations) a 50 percent rate of return was required.[44] But, the president declared: "On Class III and IV expenditures we calculate return on total capital expenditures, including working capital. Hence it is easier to get given return on I and II."[45]

Capital Supply Considerations

In regard to capital supply considerations, the assistant treasurer asserted: "We are influenced by our desired equity-debt structure and tax considerations. Any financial office would like to keep only to equity. Of course the tax structure makes that inadvisable but you don't want to get too bound if conditions change."

Probing further on the matter revealed that the desired debt and equity considerations had flexible weights, like many other norms and rules. The assistant treasurer explained: "It was generally understood that we would keep our position in the industry. If not, the fixed limit on borrowing and consequent restrictions might have been different." But the problem of keeping one's place in the industry in this context relates to expansions in capacity to match those by competitors in response to a growth in demand for the products of the industry. Thus the qualification expressed by the assistant treasurer may well be interpreted as ascribing prime importance to changes in demand.

---

[44] Two years later (1954), this was reported as 30 percent.

[45] On Class III and Class IV expenditures the "rate of additional annual return on total new investment" is the ratio of "net operating profit" ("sales" minus "cost of sales" minus "selling and administrative expense") to "total new investment." Calculation of total new investment comprises "raw materials and supplies inventory, goods in process inventory, finished goods inventory, accounts receivable and appropriation amount [for capital expenditure]." Rates of return are not calculated on Class I expenditures, according to Document A. On Class II expenditures the ratio is simply "estimated annual saving" (which would correspond to "net operating profit" on Class III and Class IV) to "appropriation amount." The president's remark would appear somewhat misleading, however, except in a purely arithmetical sense, since Class II expenditures would presumably not require net additions to working capital. Hence, failure to require a return on working capital in the case of Class II expenditures is hardly a discrimination in their favor.

Taxes and the Rate of Interest

On the subject of taxes and interest cost the president observed that the interest rate on borrowing was probably *not* negative since "we are bumping the ceiling and hence not showing a steady profiting." However, he added, "Even with no [special] tax advantage, the interest rate is much less than without taxes." This last suggests another factor reducing the significance of interest cost (although, of course, it should apply equally to all current costs incurred in the hope of gain in a future period when taxes may be less or may have a different incidence).

Accelerated Amortization

Although it does not request that depreciation charges be included generally in calculations of expected profitability of new assets, Document A does declare:

> Whenever accelerated depreciation is allowed or will be applied for ... by filing a formal application of certificate of necessity, the rate of return on the total new investment shall be calculated and shown on the request, both on the basis of including and excluding such accelerated depreciation.

Charging the accelerated depreciation will reduce sharply the nominal or accounting profits, before taxes, that can be expected in the years immediately ahead. But since company officers were well aware that rapidly amortized property would, in many (if not most) cases, prove profitable for long years after the period of amortization, it seemed desirable to indicate the more profitable appearance offered by charging only normal depreciation.

This specific mention of accelerated amortization, whatever its immediate implications, suggests that amortization possibilities influence investment decisions. Such an influence is confirmed by the president, who said: "Of course 50 per cent return is 15 per cent net (of taxes). We give a lot of thought on certificates of necessity and they play a major role in our capital expenditure decisions."

Flexibility and Time Lags

Document A declared, "On major projects involving extensive engineering and costing over $300,000, an appropriation request may be submitted for approval in principle of funds in advance of detailed engineering cost estimates." It adds:

> The use of the *Approval in Principle* request is intended to apply to projects that must be scheduled over an extended period of time, either because of the complexity of the work involved or because of the size of the proj-

ect. It is intended to apply to long-range facility improvements and major expansion programs. Approval of such requests constitutes authority to proceed with engineering and preparation of cost estimates. No commitments shall be made or money spent before funds have been approved on a specific request applicable to the *Approval in Principle.*

As detailed engineering cost estimates are developed, specific requests applicable to the project shall be submitted. The total of the specific requests shall not exceed the amount approved in principle.

This may be taken to suggest the existence of a substantial period, with reference to large projects, when expenditures may be halted after initial decisions have been favorable and little or no investment has actually been made. Further evidence of flexibility may be seen in a statement by the assistant treasurer that "A sudden change in the business outlook could cause us to change plans either by acceleration or delay of forward capital expenditure plans."

Accuracy of Estimates

Document A also declares:

An expenditure of not more than 10 per cent over and not more than 20 per cent under the amount approved on a specific request shall be considered as within the authorized limits of the original approval. . . . As soon as it is evident that the cost to complete the work as detailed will be in excess of 10 per cent over the amount requested, a supplementary request shall be presented in the usual manner for approval . . .

When the additional funds requested exceed 50 per cent of the original amount approved, the request, regardless of the amount, shall in all cases be submitted to the Executive Committee for approval.

These procedures may suggest that lesser officials requesting expenditures are likely to overestimate their needs to avoid having to run the gantlet of measures necessary for securing supplementary authorizations. To the extent that such overestimates would be reflected in anticipations of aggregate capital expenditures by the firm, these procedures might thus lead to anticipations in excess of the expenditures that occur. However, any such tendency may be balanced by several other elements in the procedures. For one thing, the higher the estimate of expenditures required, the lower, other things being equal, will be the estimated rate of return and hence the greater may be the difficulty of meeting the earnings criterion necessary for approval. Secondly, the procedure provides explicitly for underruns, as follows: "An explanation shall be made on Form . . . outlining the reasons when actual expenditures are more than 20 per cent less than the total amount approved. Copies of [this] Form . . . shall be routed to the level of authority approving the original request . ." It is of course hardly possible to judge definitively the effect on balance of these various factors on the accuracy of forward estimates of capital expenditures. We may, however, suggest that there is nothing indicated herein which seems to damage seriously the hypothesis suggested earlier that pressures of intra-firm relations are such that management personnel on the whole will prefer to overestimate rather than underestimate expenditures. Whether overestimates actually occur will depend as well, of course, on a host of other factors.[46]

In regard to specific capital expenditure surveys, the assistant treasurer, with the finance chairman concurring, said:

On [a particular national capital expenditures survey], due to the indefiniteness of their questions, if others' answers are like ours, I would not be too confident about the quality. — We generally do a fairly good job on [this survey]. Of course, it's difficult when you don't see them personally to know what the questions mean.

---

[46] In a comment on a draft of this section, however, an officer of the company wrote: "The suggestion or inference given in the paragraph [above] is not supported by experience. Of necessity, all estimates given on appropriation requests must be as accurate as possible. Any series or combination of sizeable over or underruns would be severely criticized, and would lead to serious question as to the ability of the authority proposing the appropriation.

Our recent experience has been, of over 1000 projects of all classes only 5% require the submission of explanation for underruns or for specific request to cover overruns."

In another letter to the interviewer this officer wrote that, aside from the results of "a sudden change in the business outlook," "our one and two year forward capital expenditure plans generally come fairly close to original planning. Frequently, there may be switches in some projects (that is, certain appropriations being dropped and others substituted), but on the whole the total is closely realized."

CPSIA information can be obtained at www.ICGtesting.com
Printed in the USA
BVOW022143160513

320955BV00002B/2/P